# I AM ENOUGH

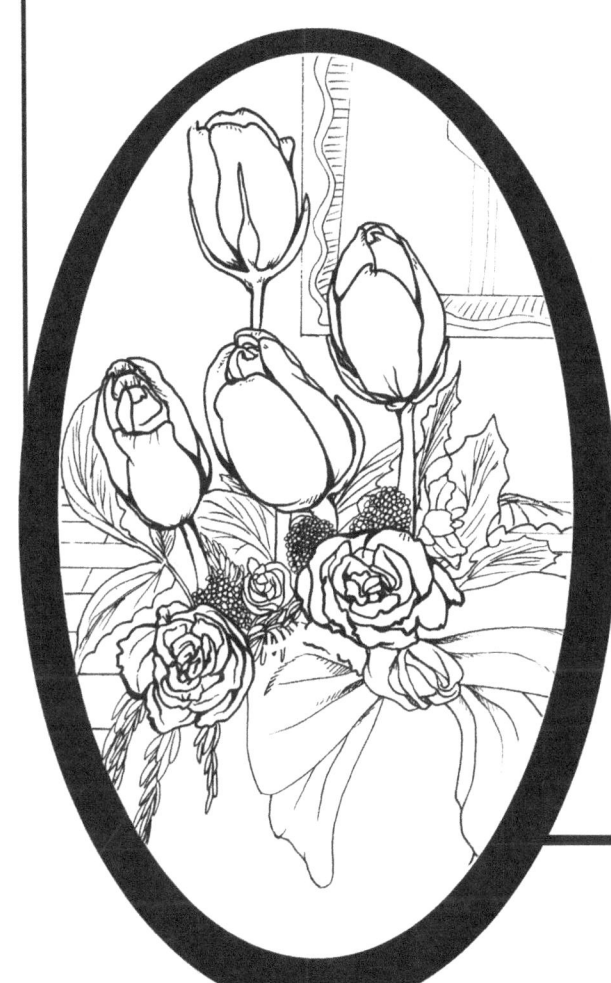

A
JOURNEY
TO
SELF WORTH

ILLUSTRATED BY

ALEXIS REEHILL

For those on
the Journey of Self-Acceptance,

I wish you all the love in the world.
May you find support and comfort
soon in your future.

# I AM ENOUGH

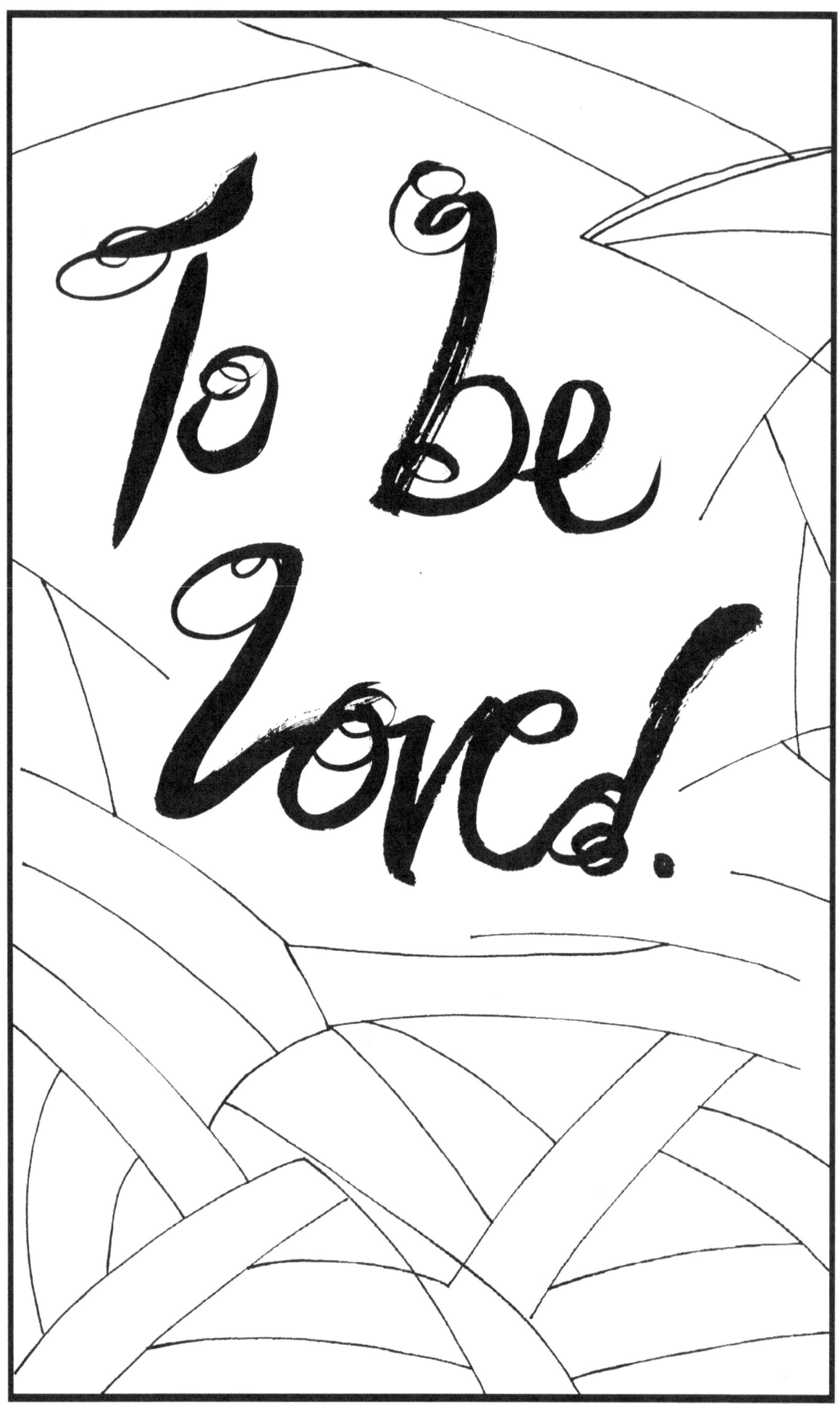

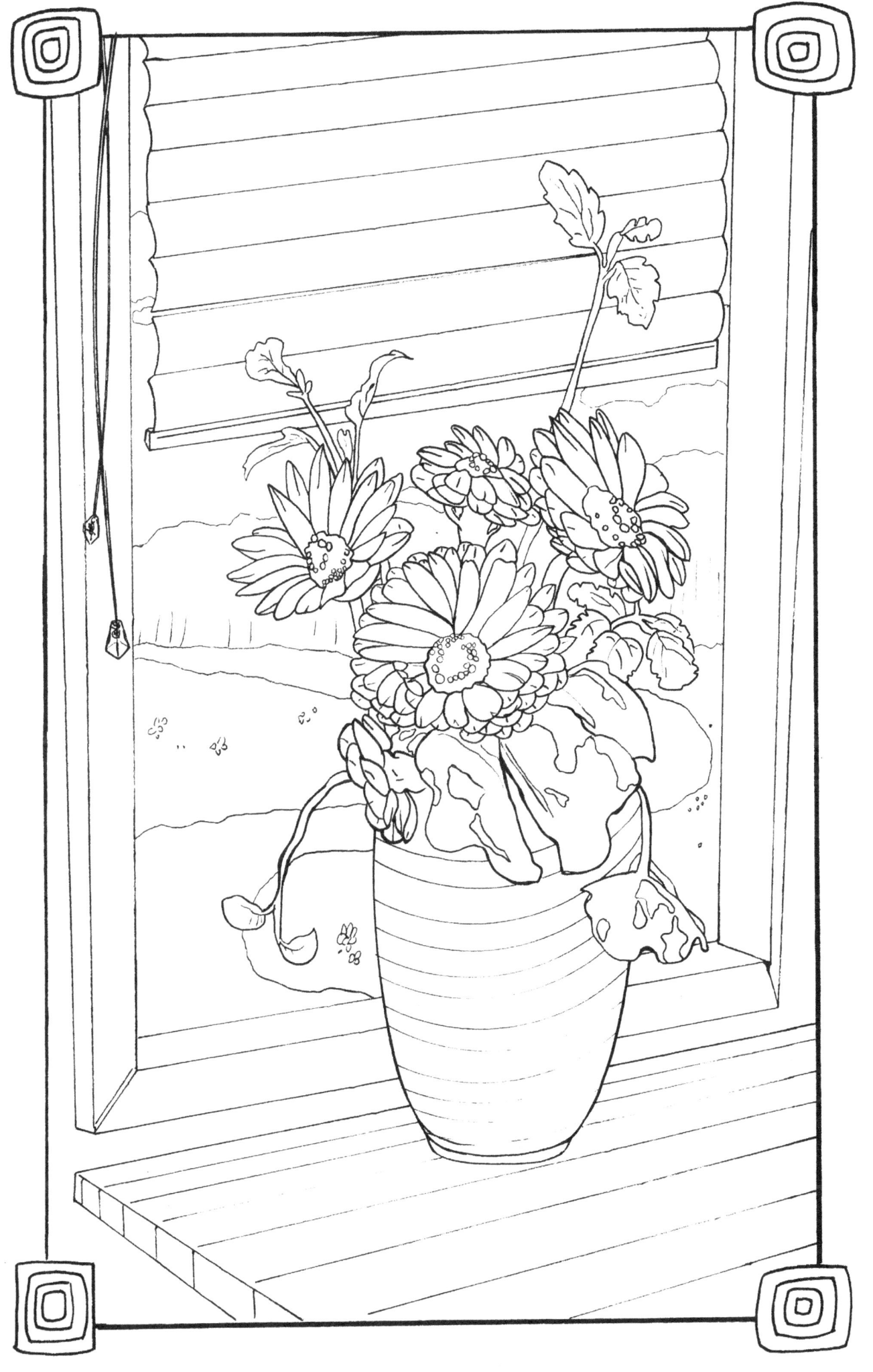

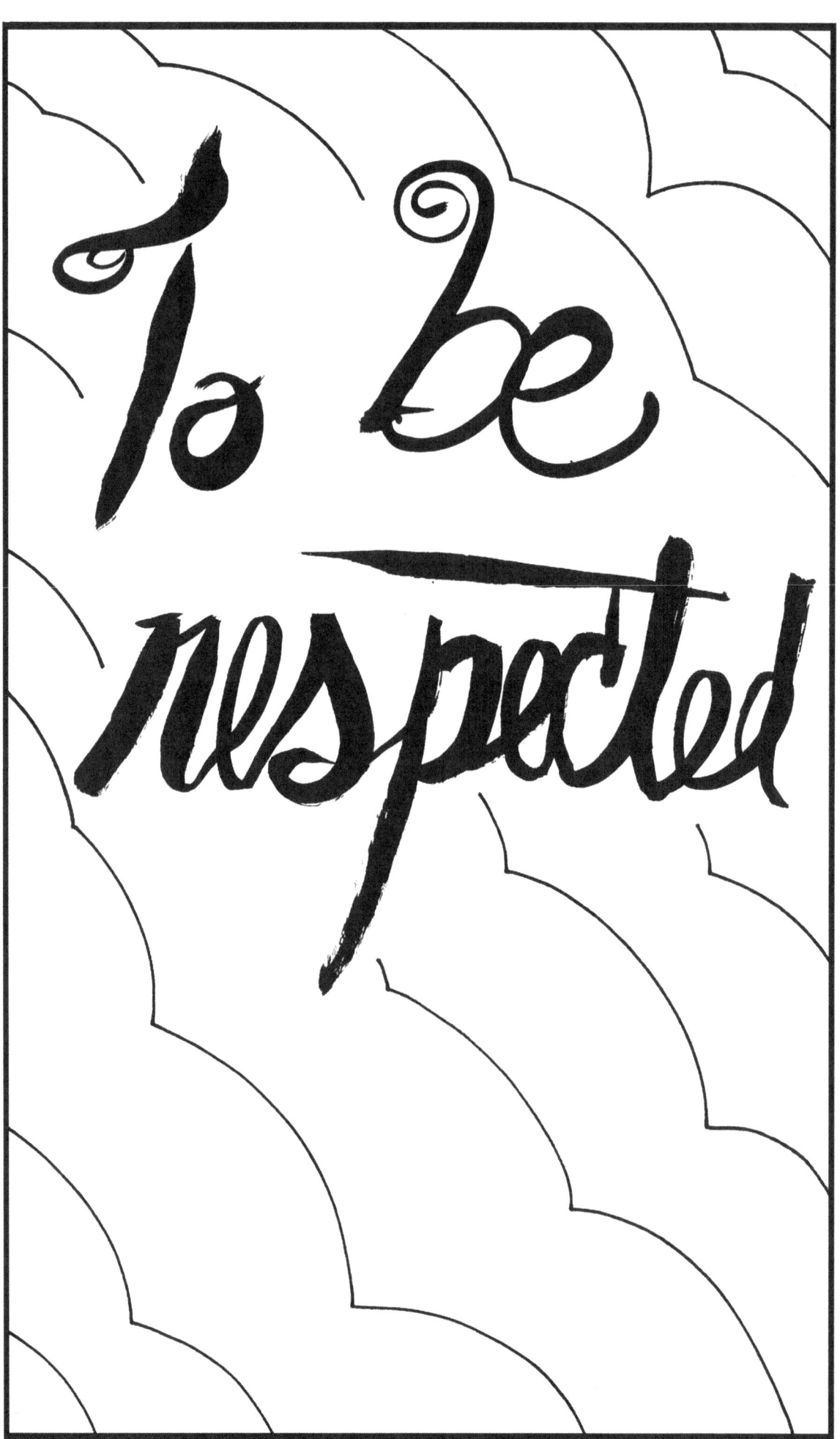

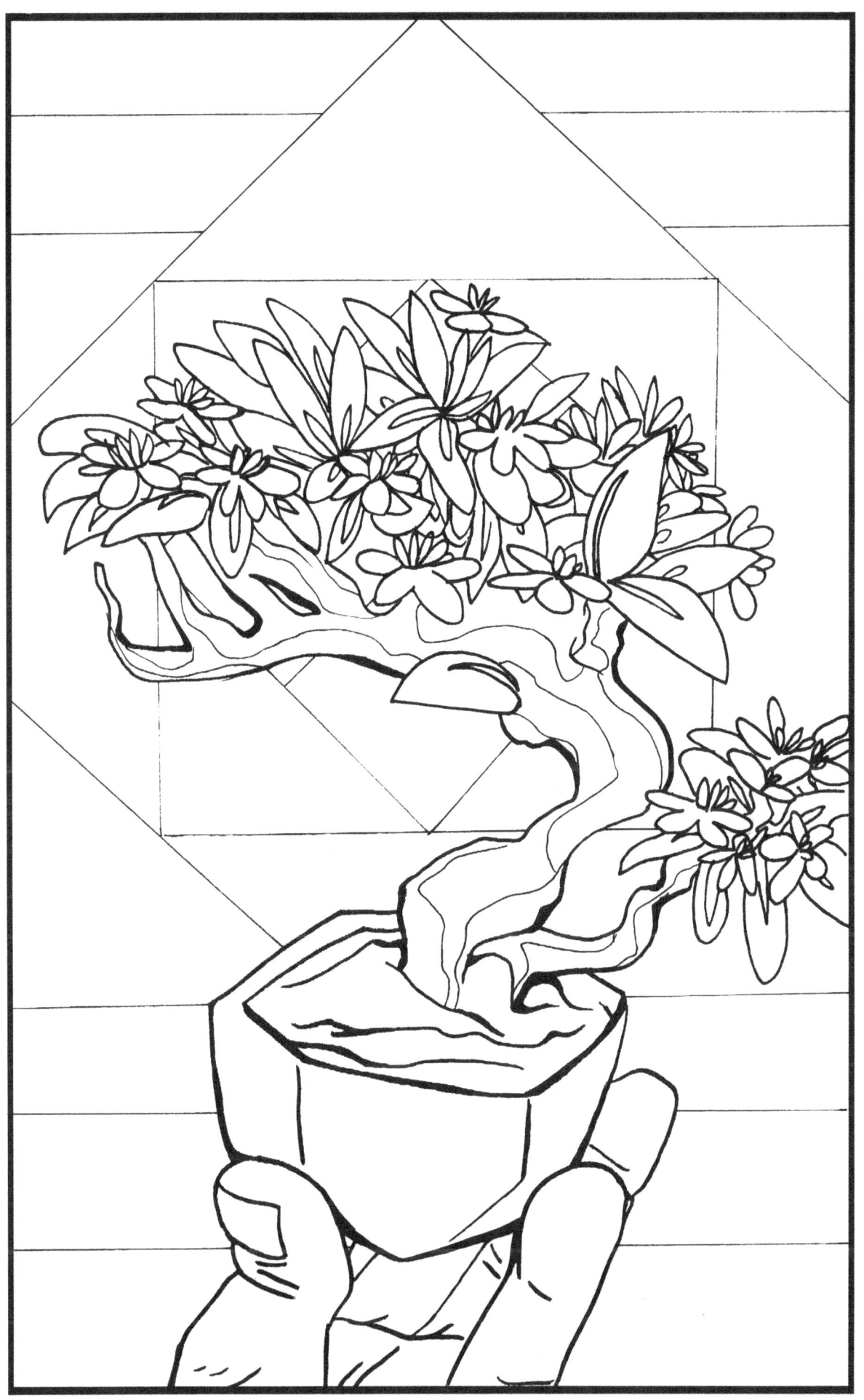

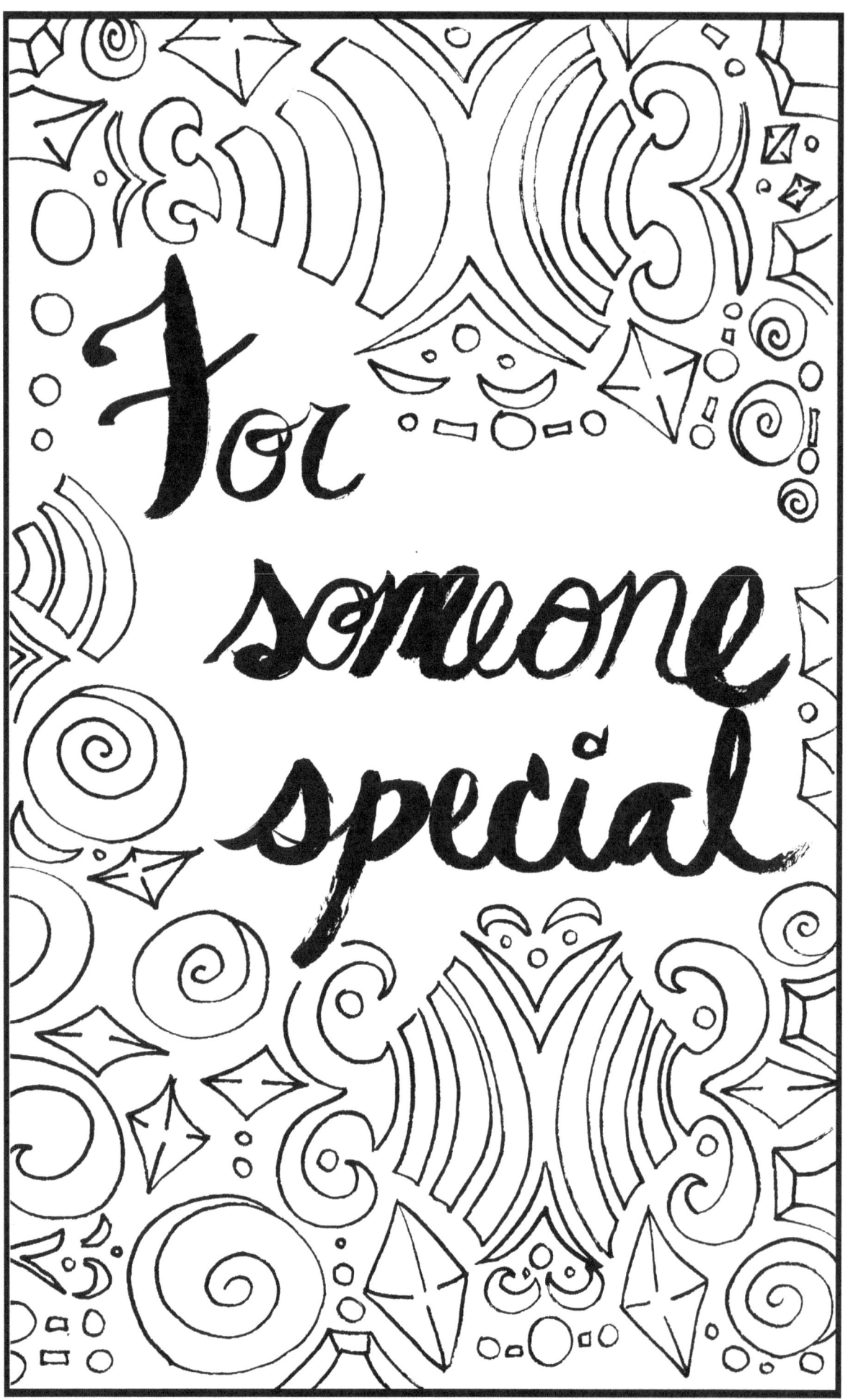

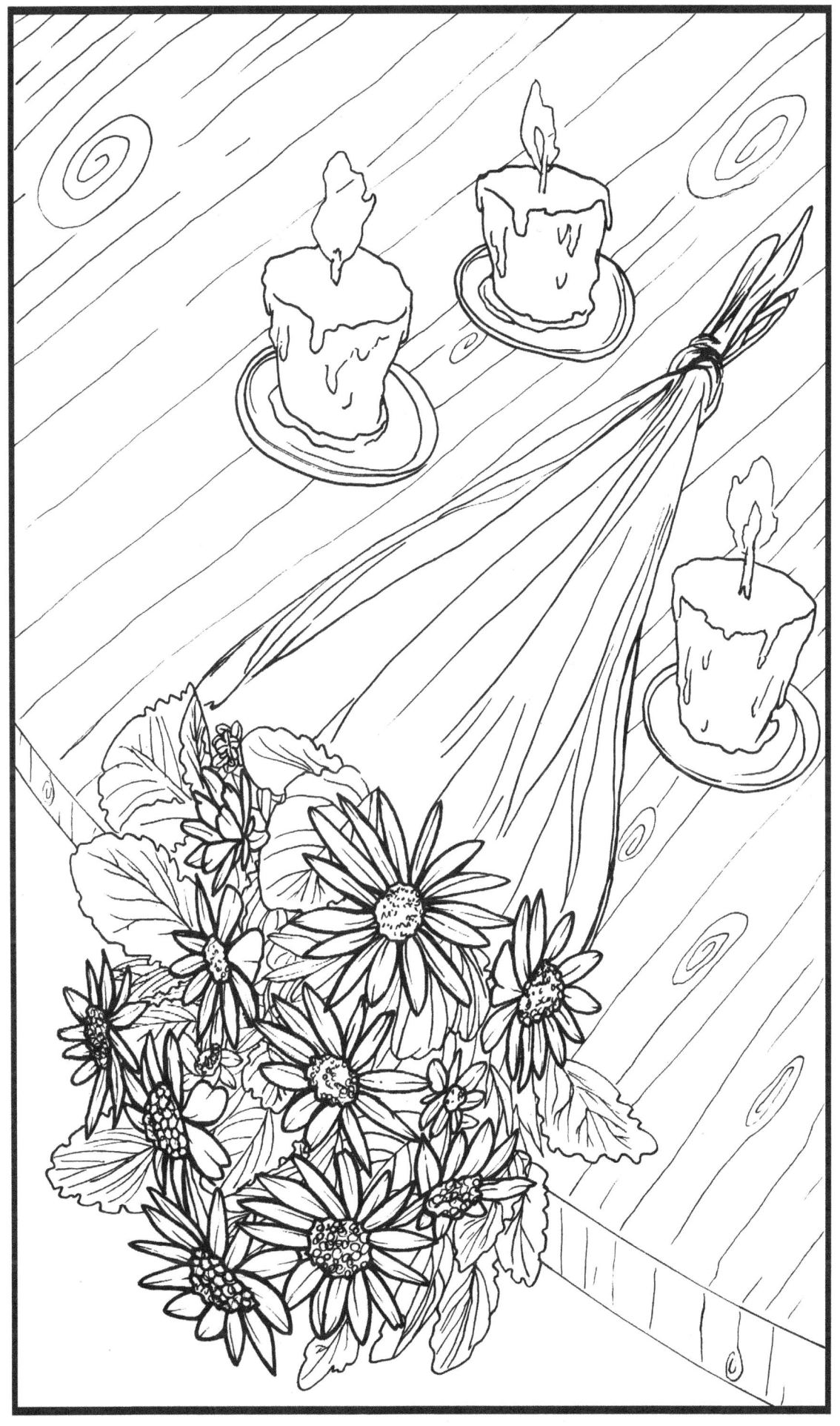

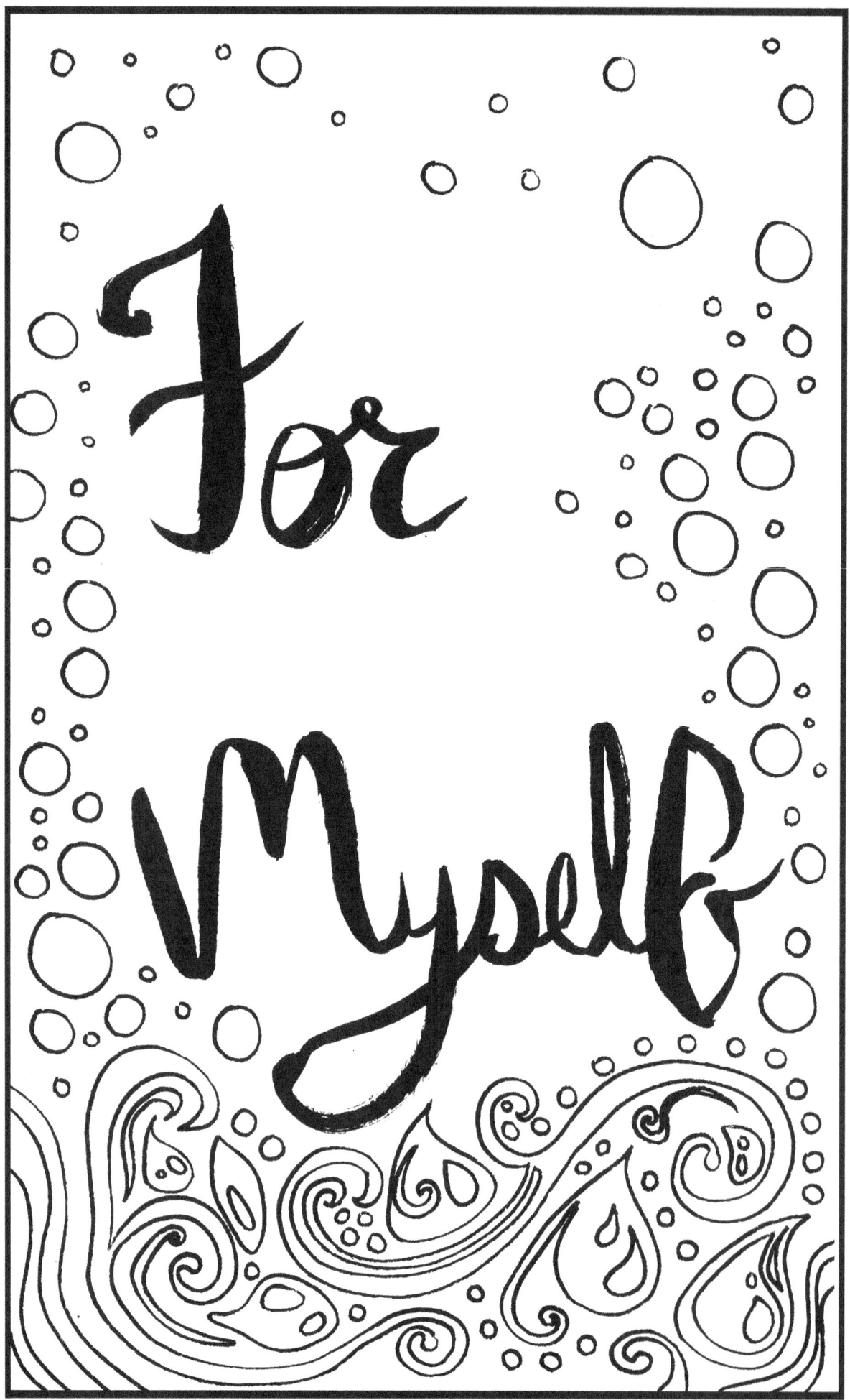

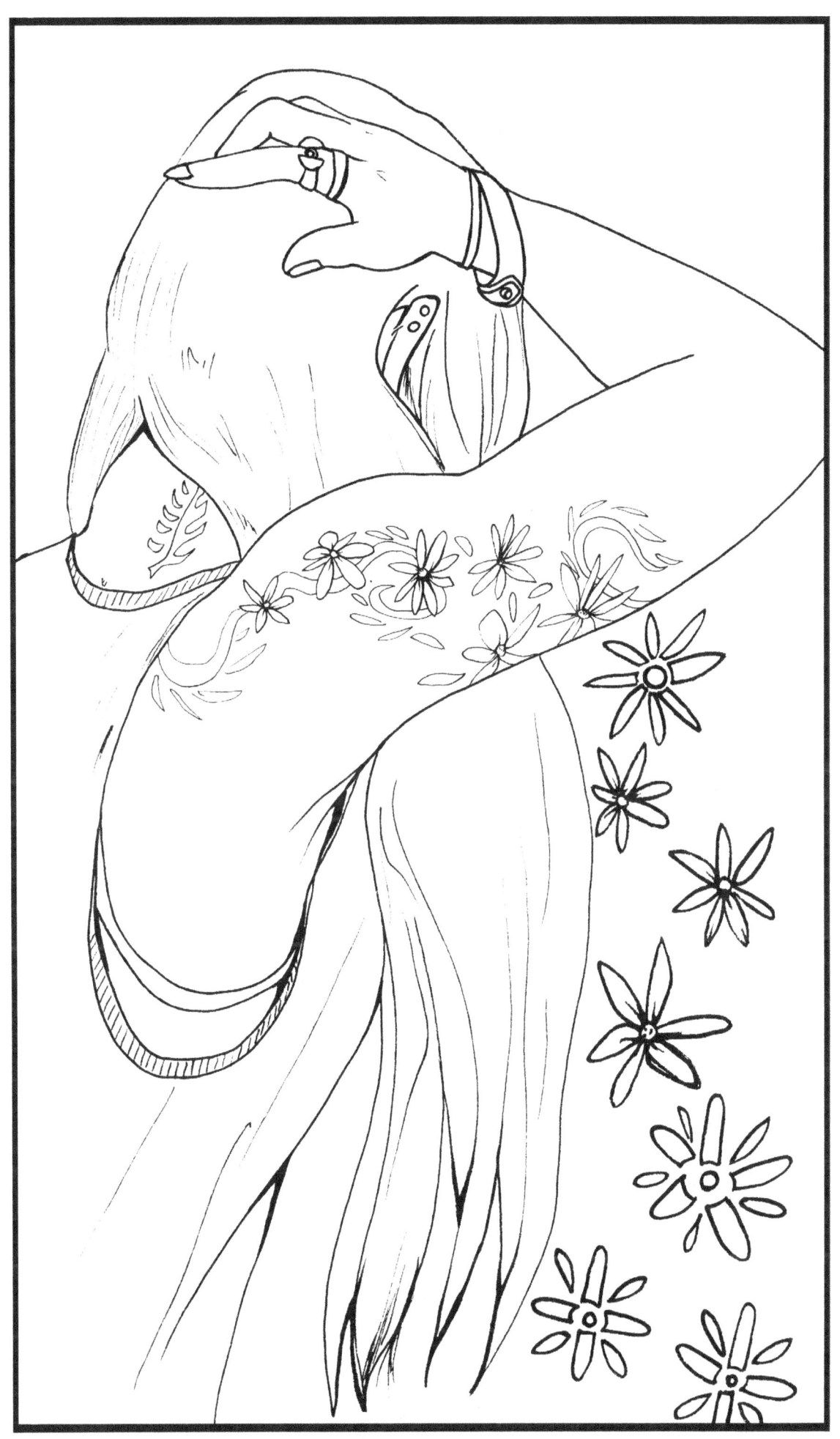

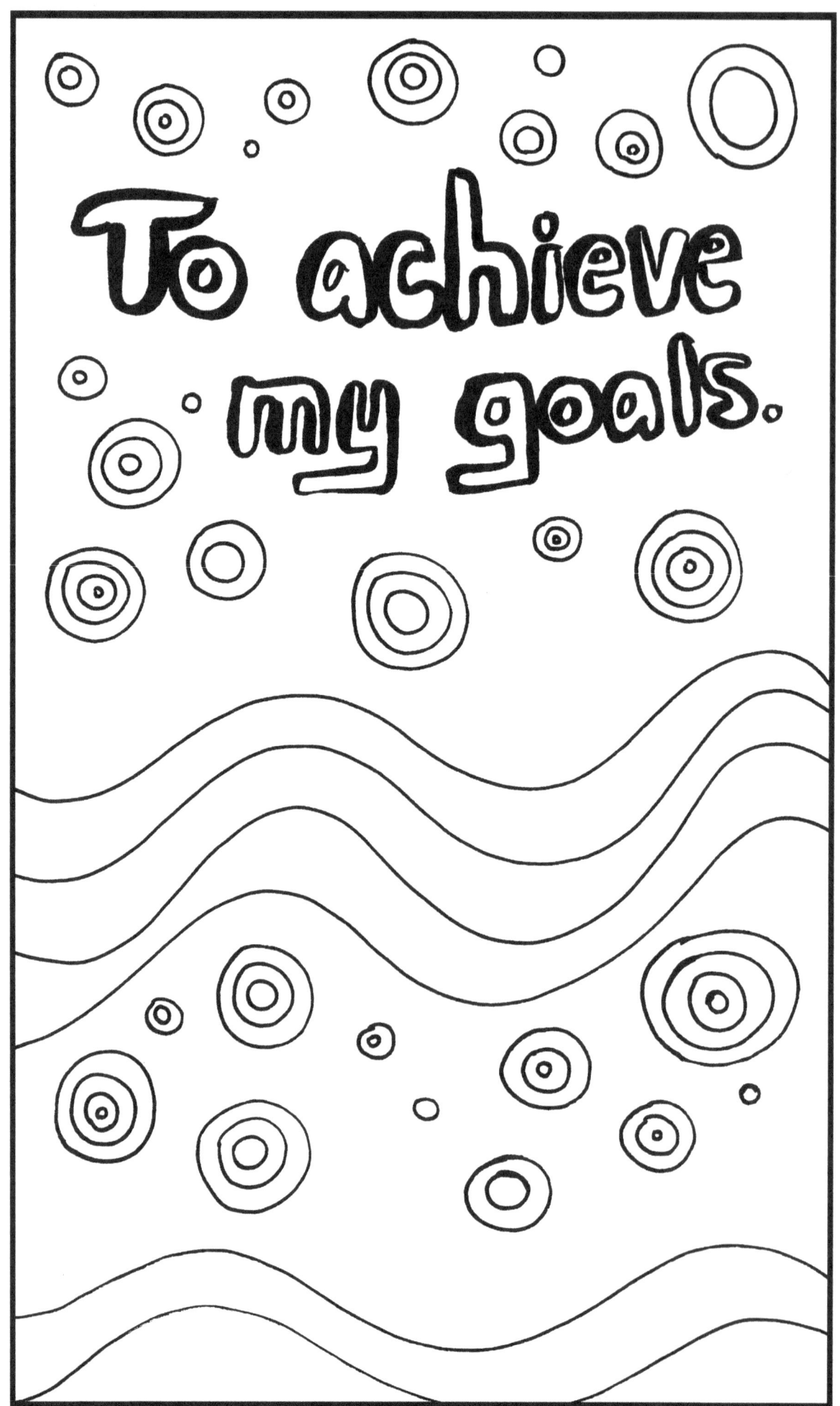

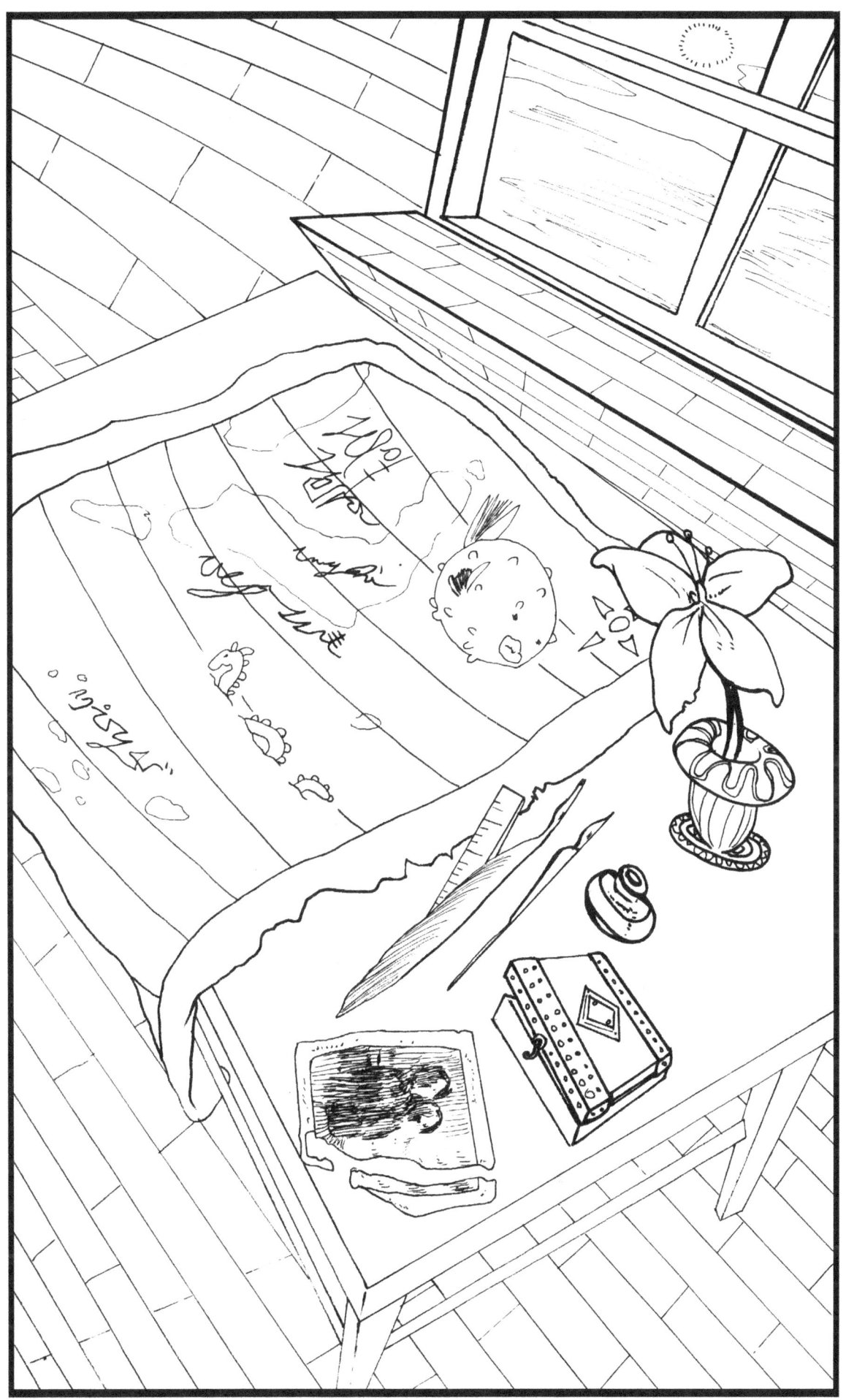

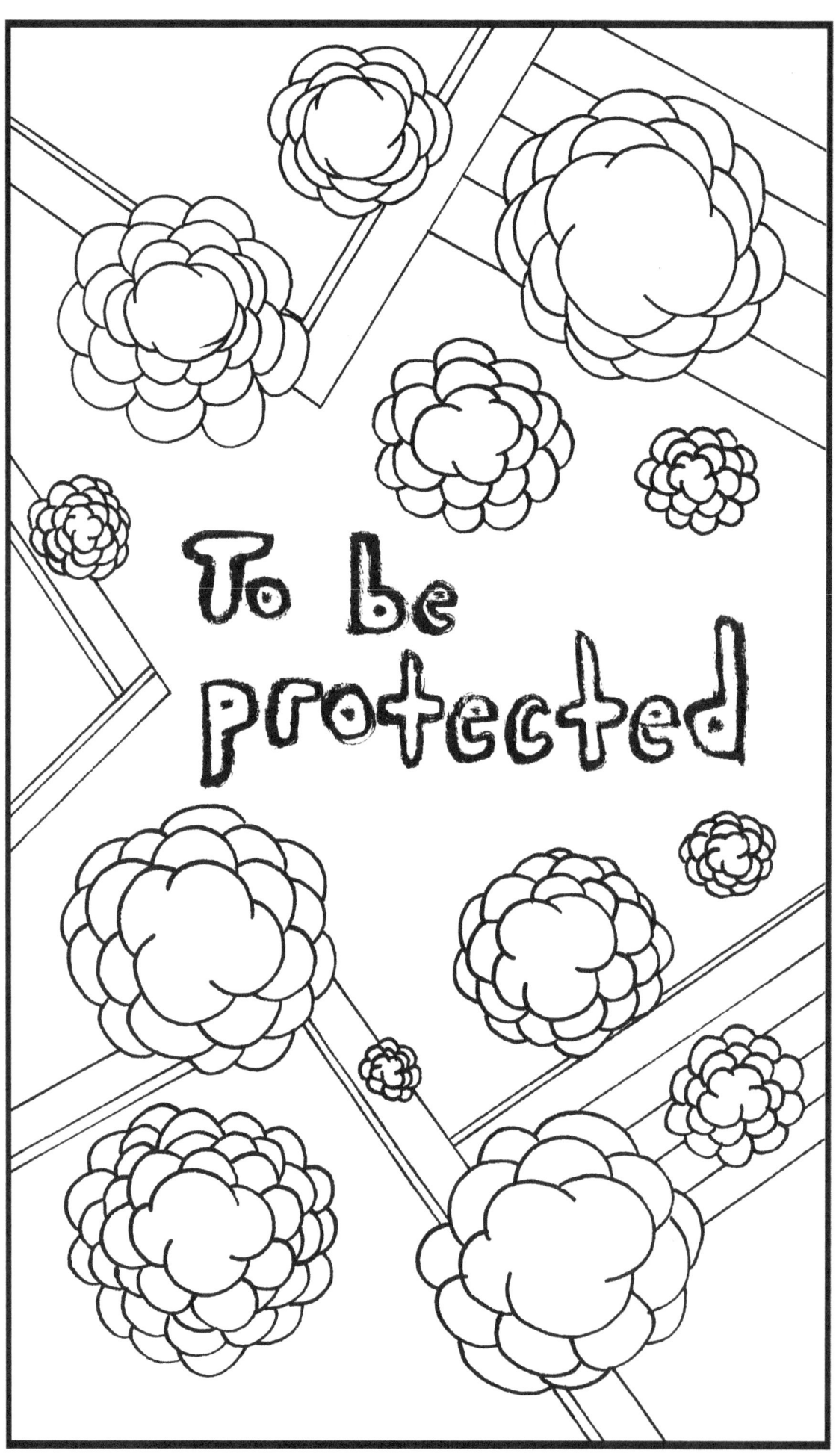

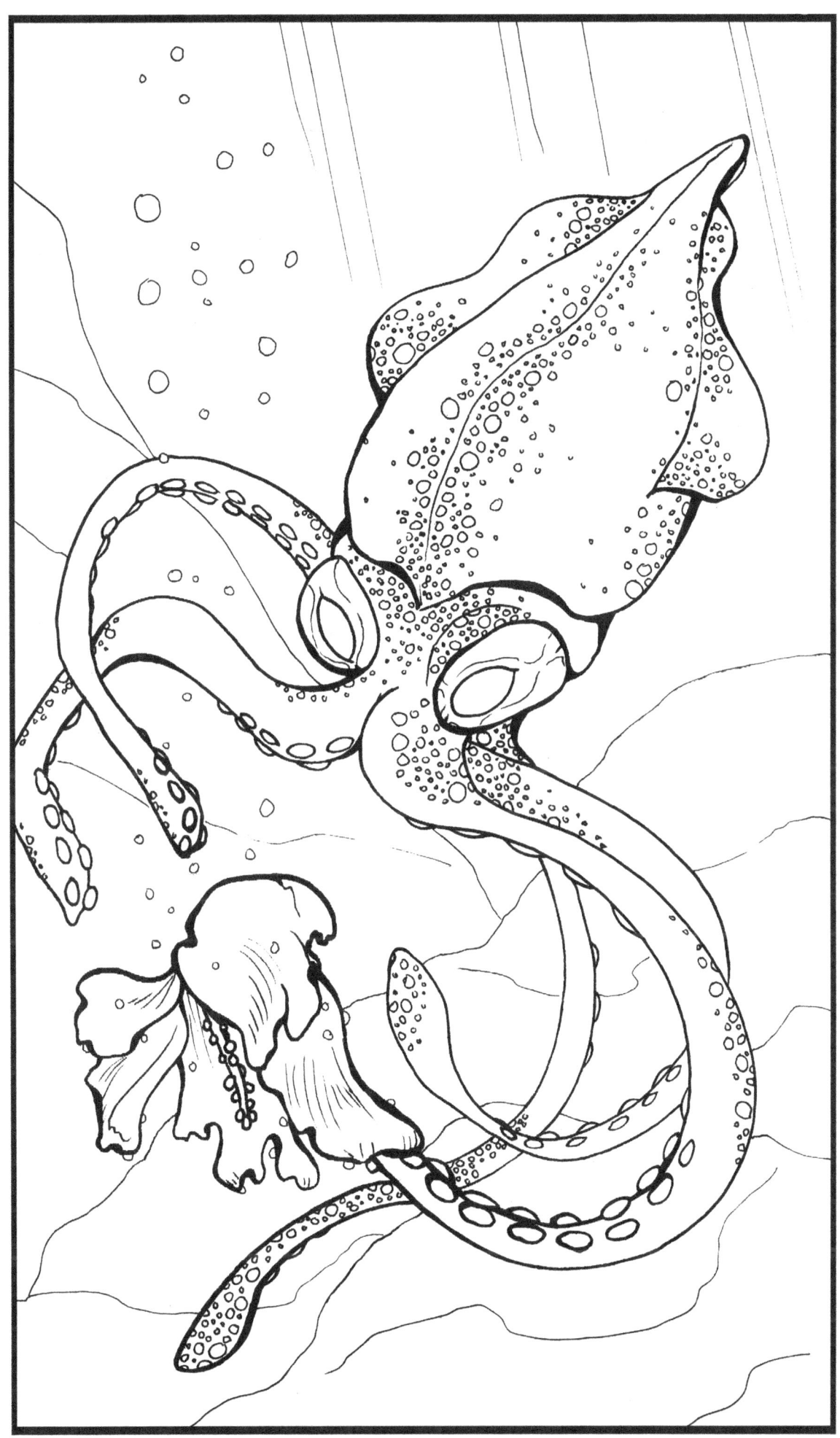

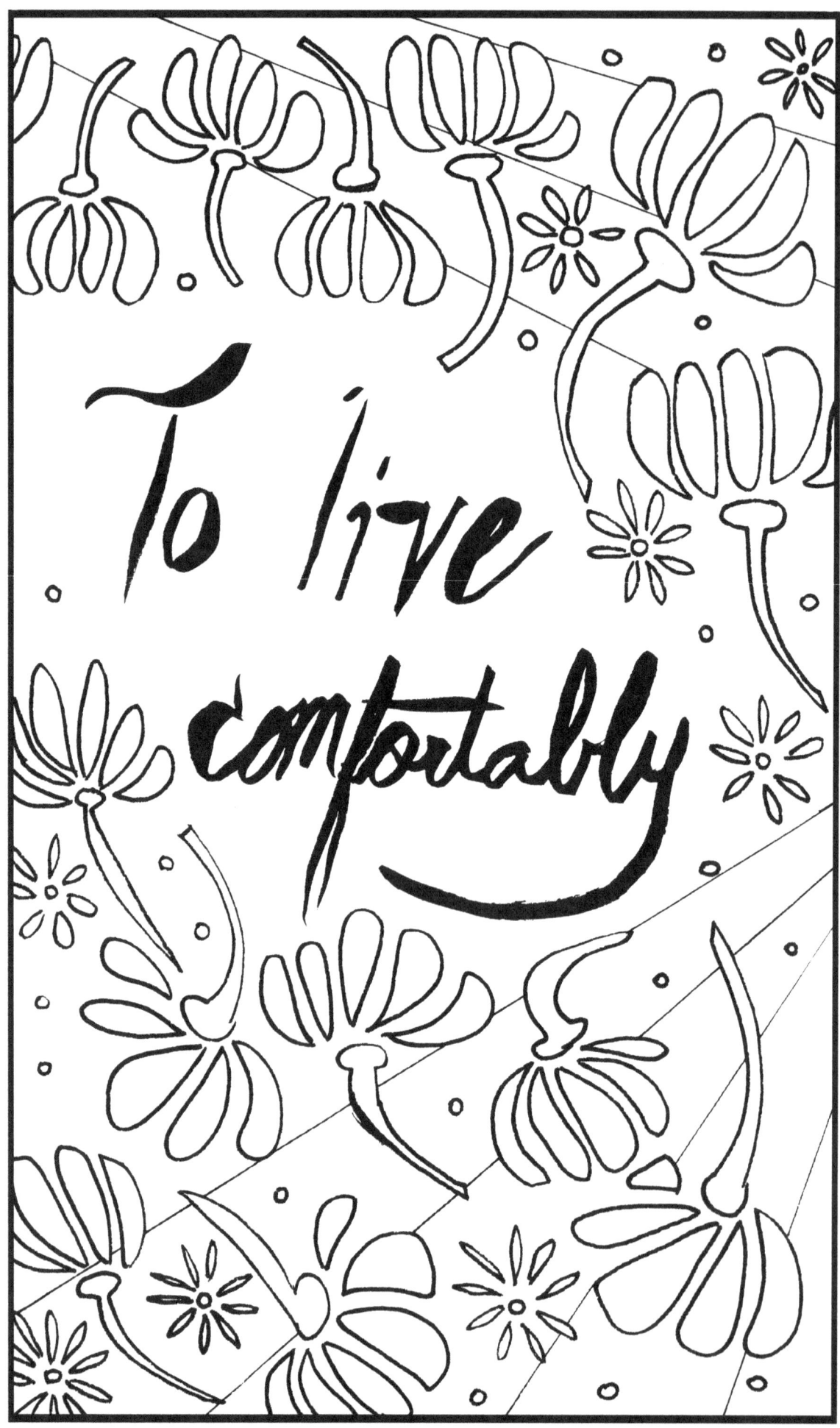

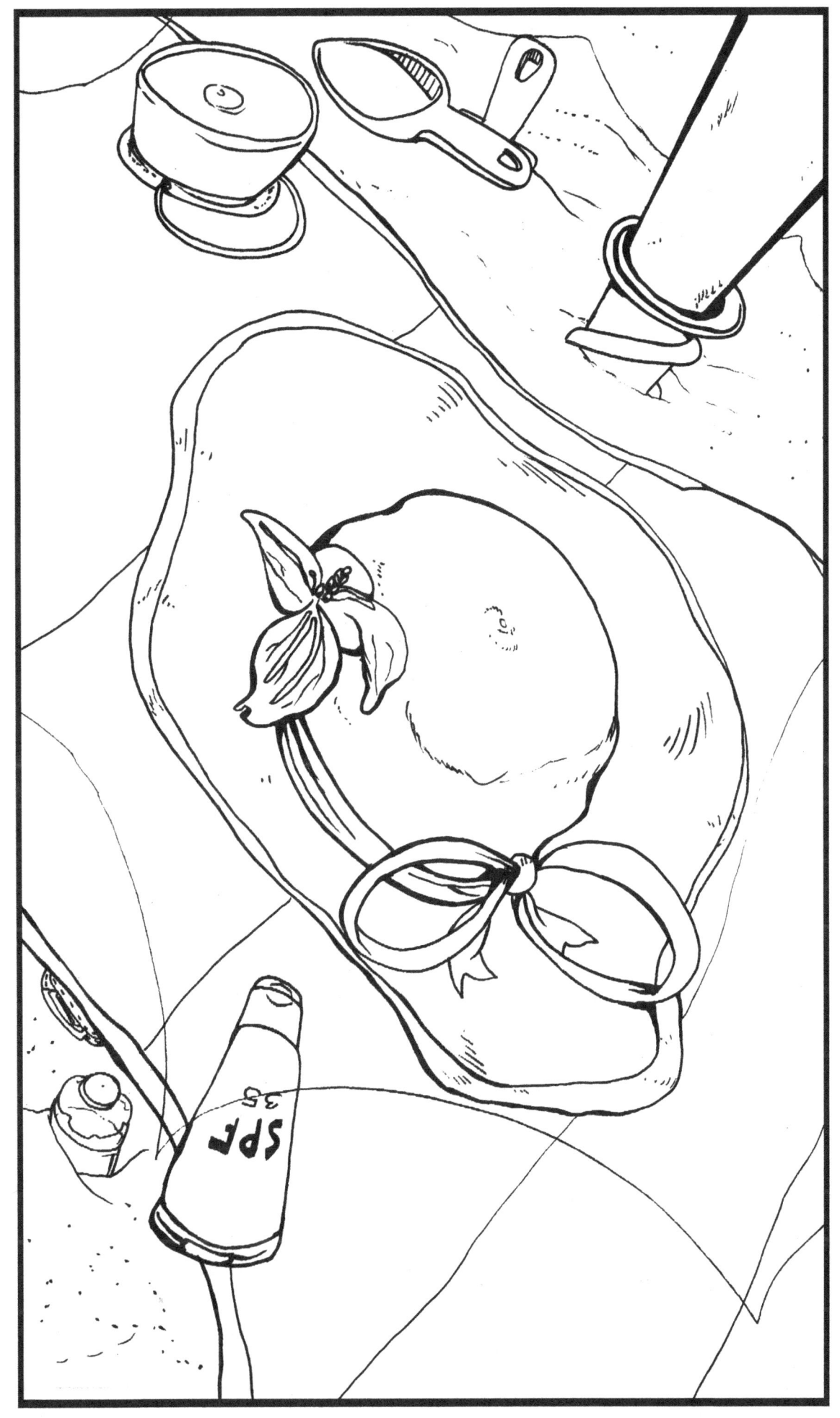

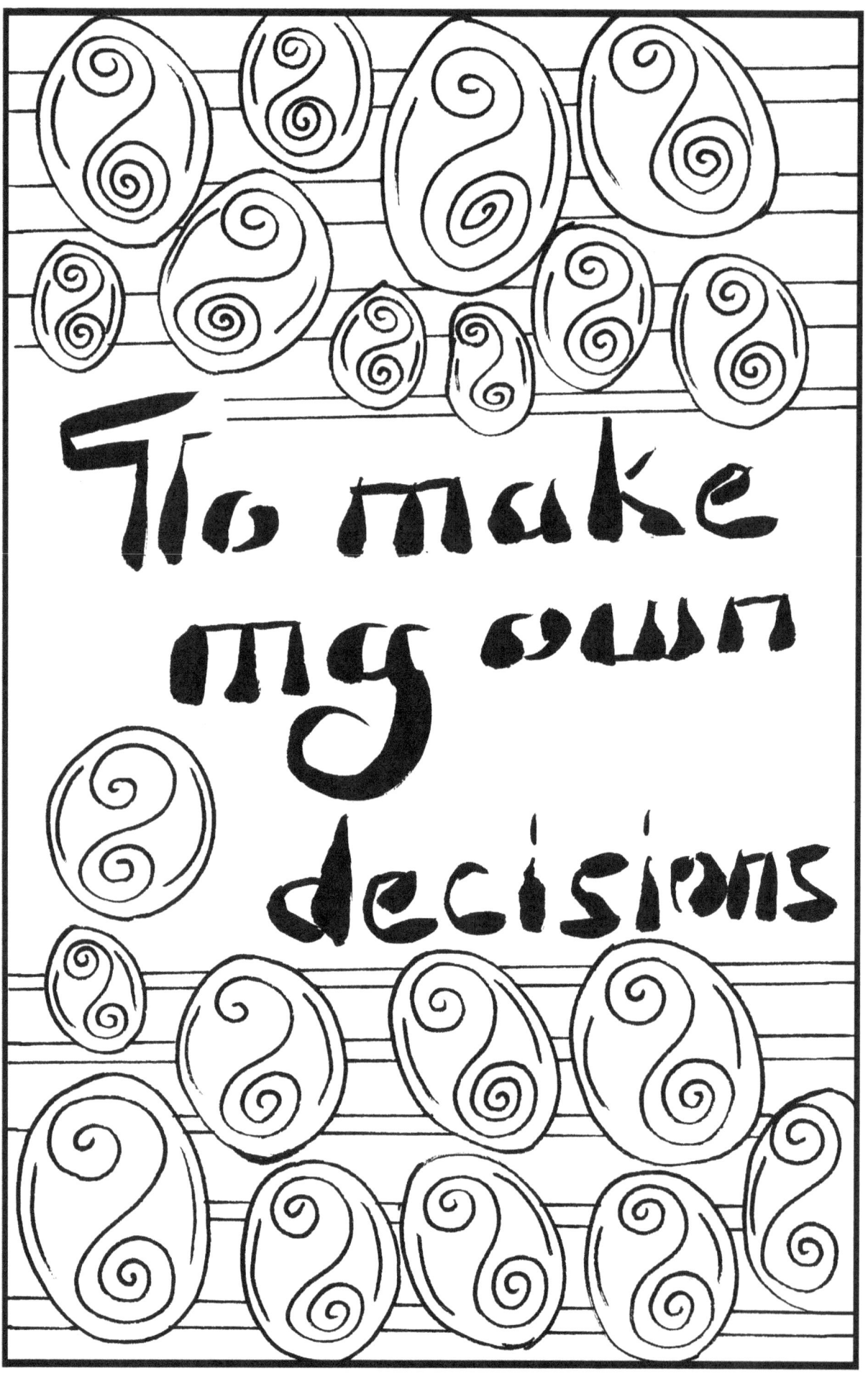

To make my own decisions

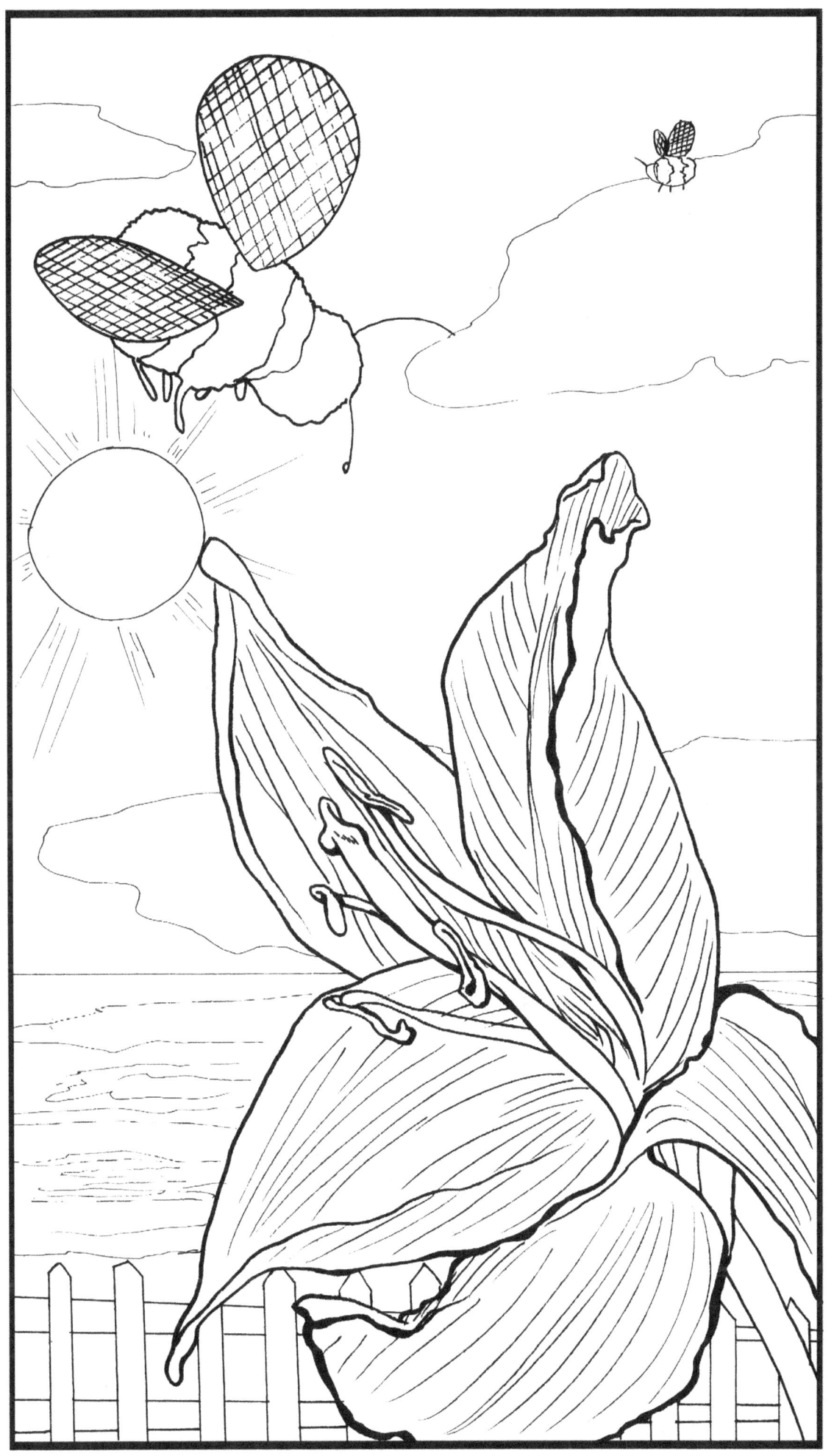

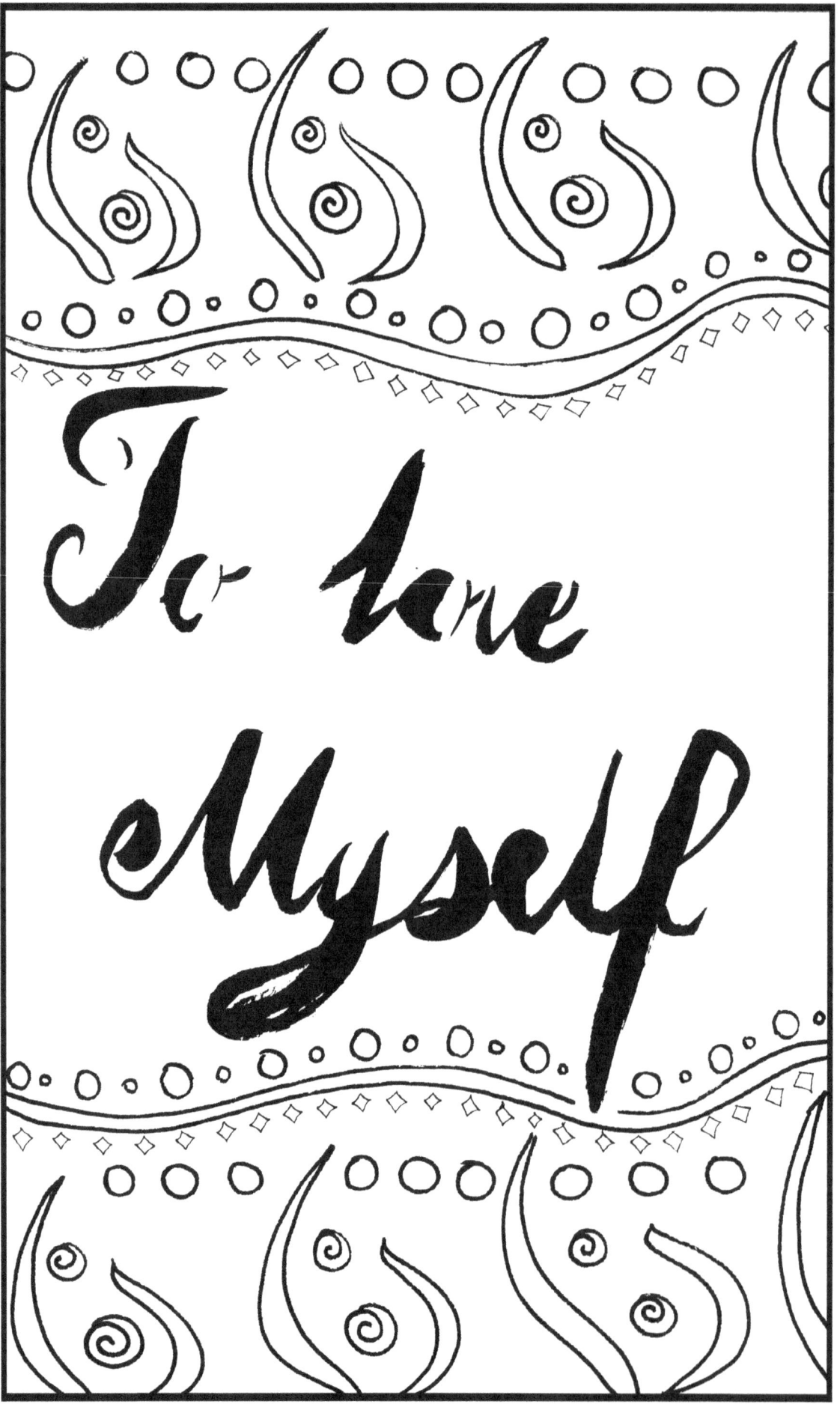

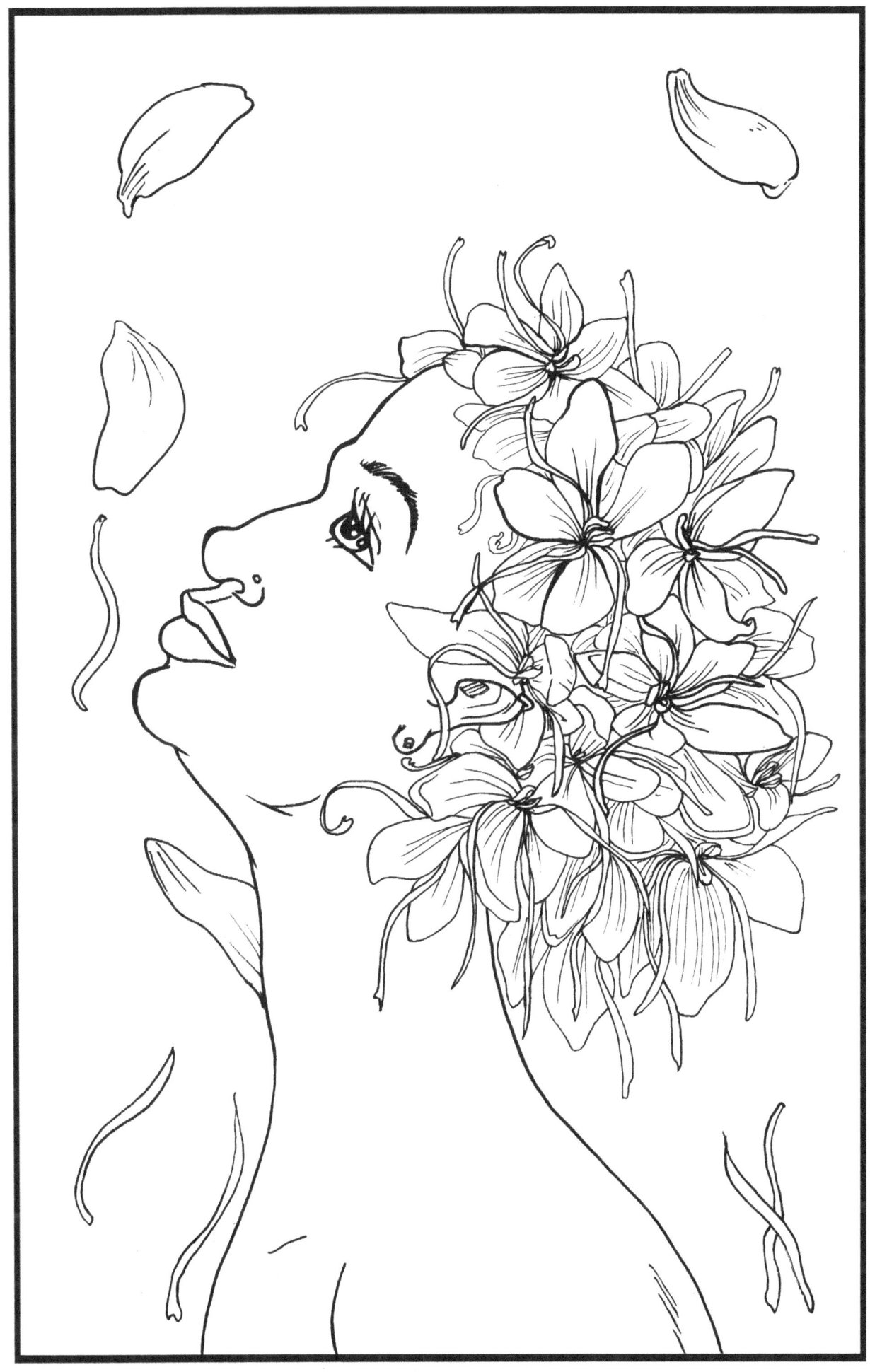

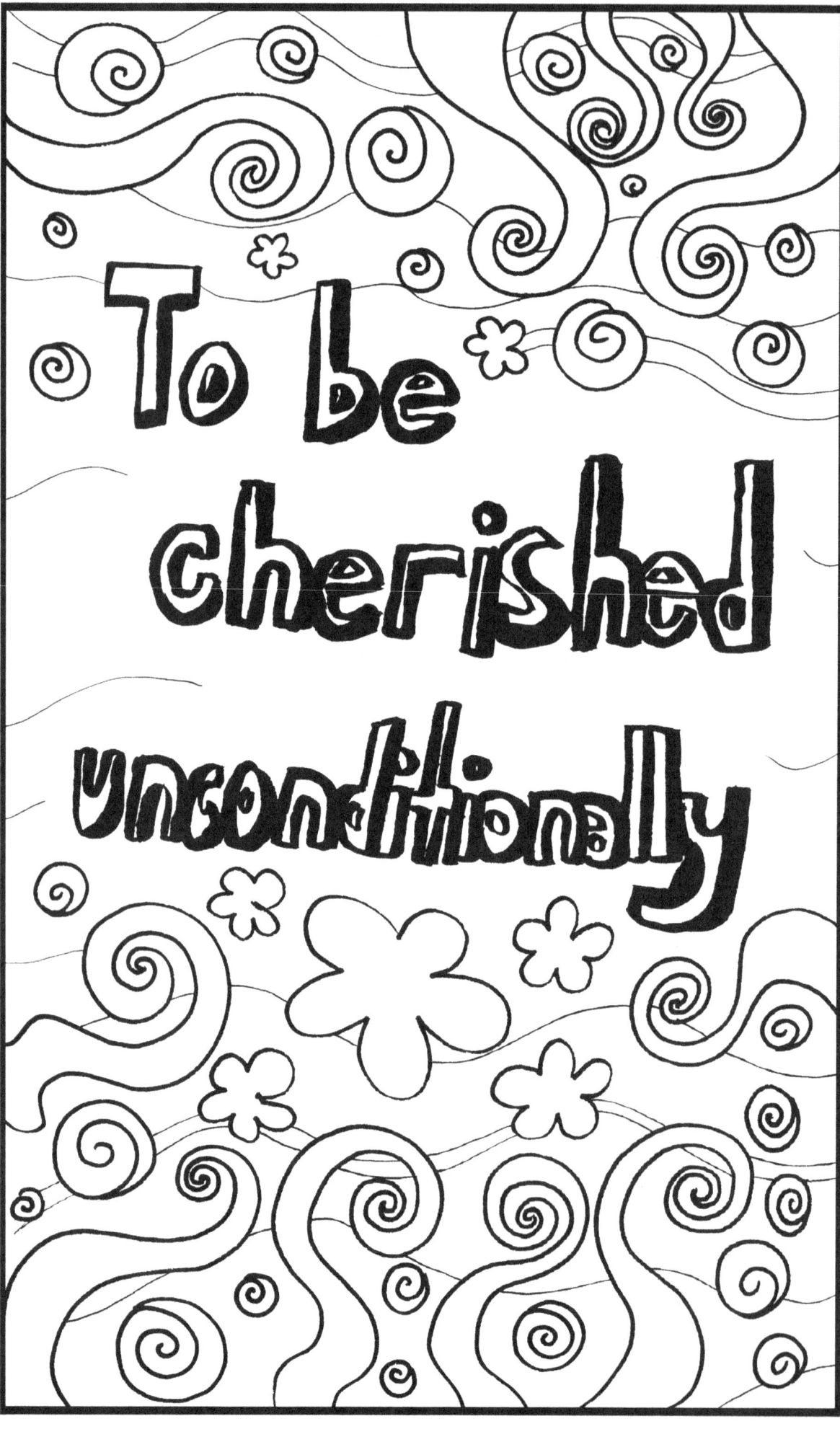

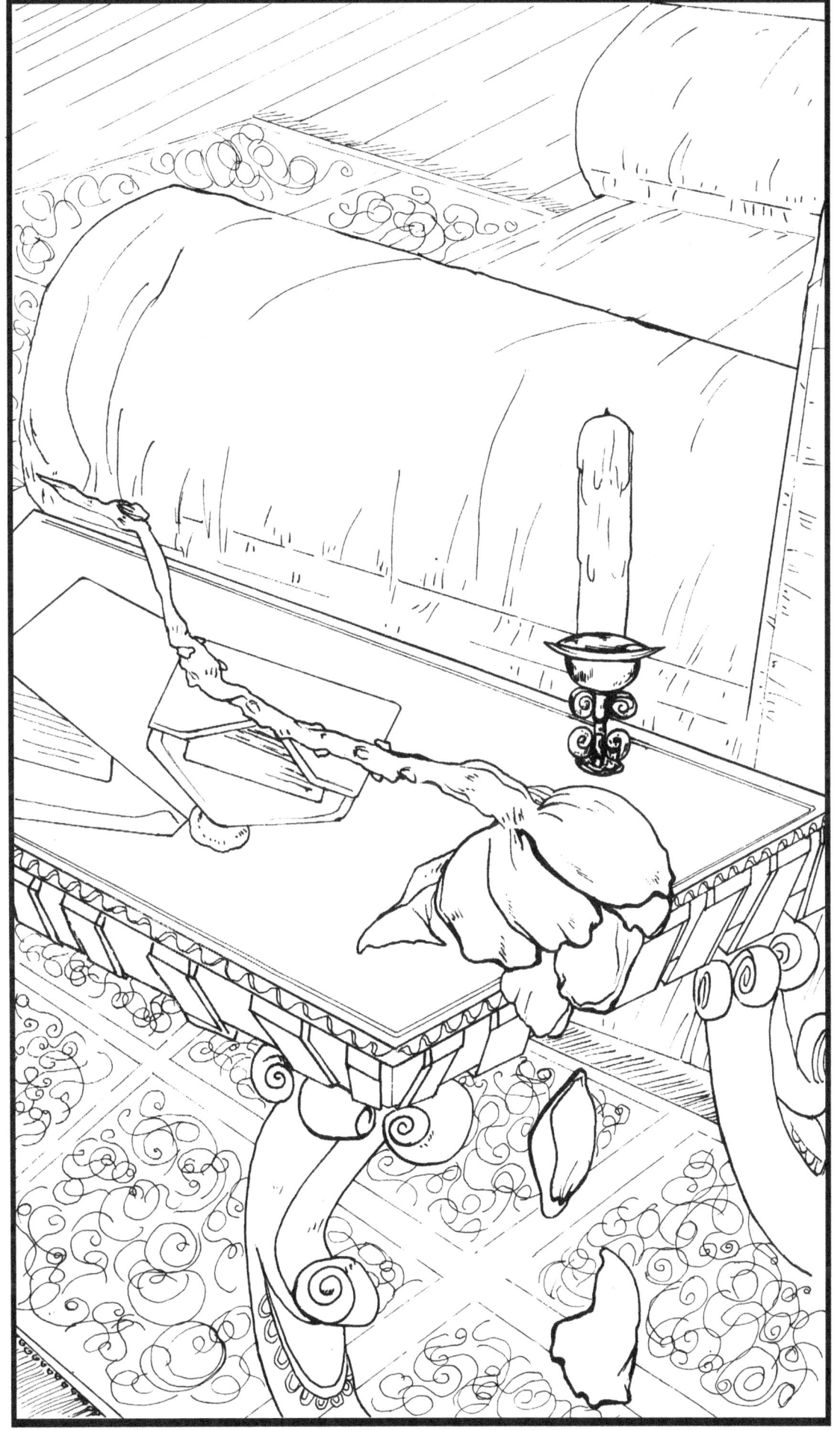

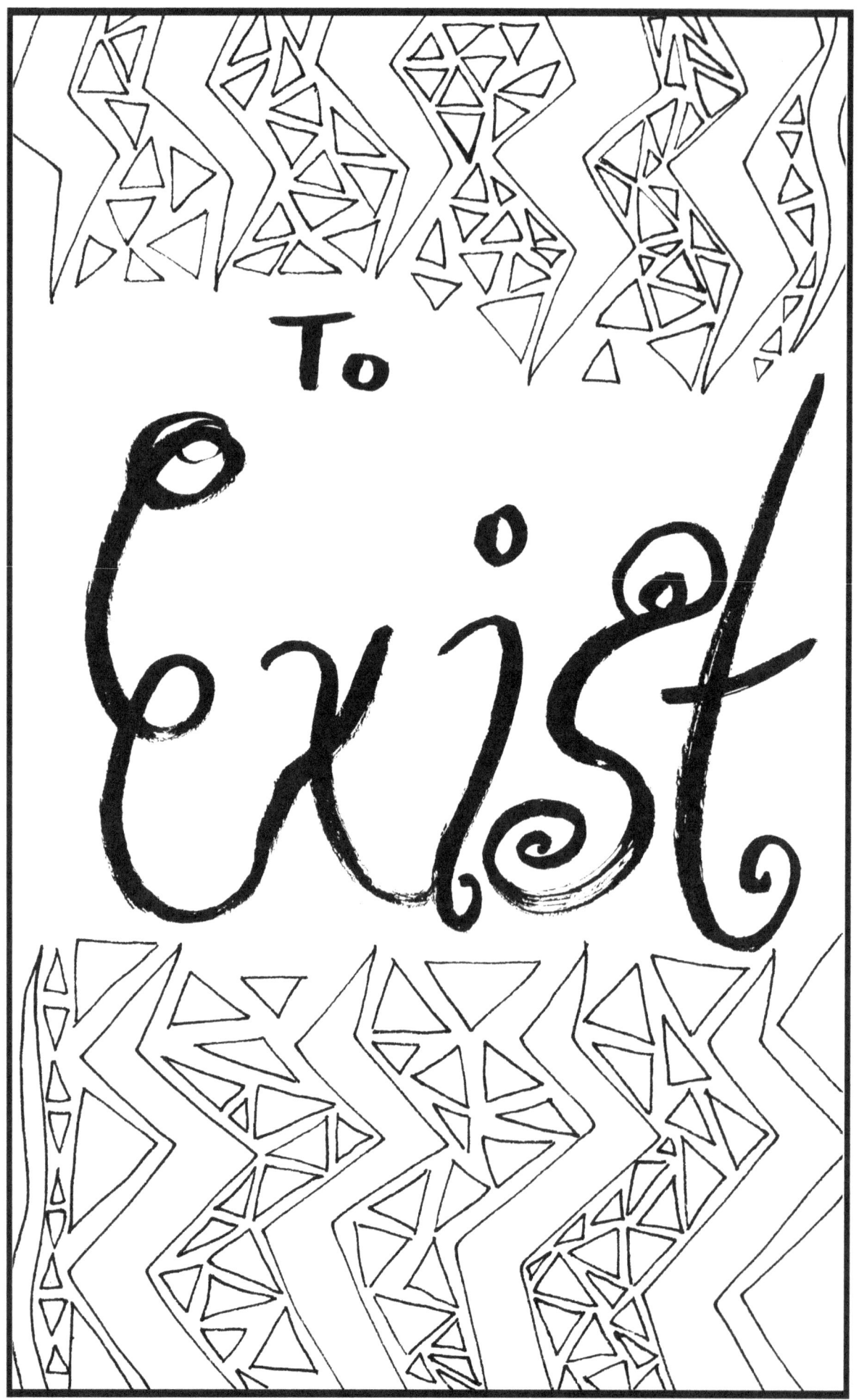

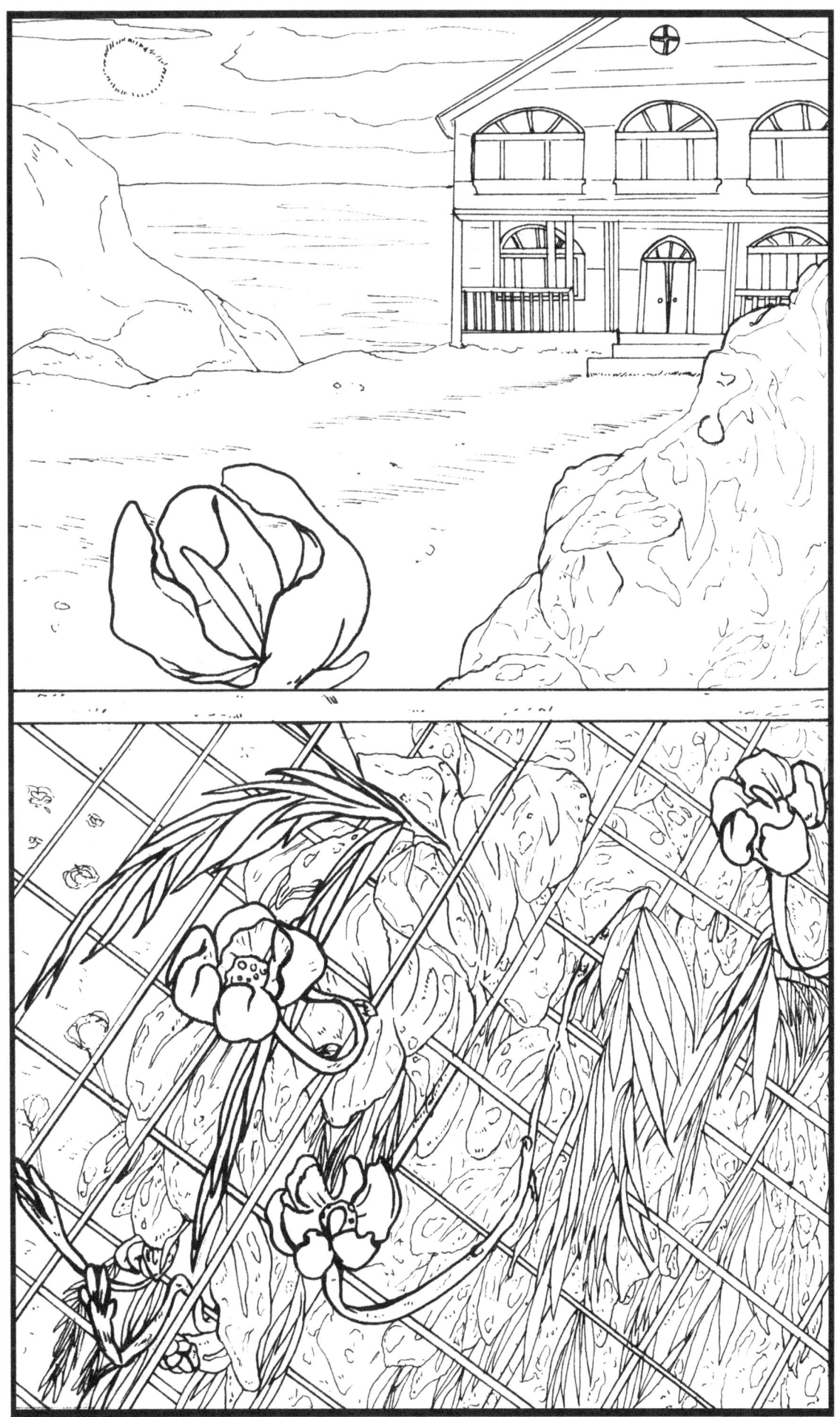

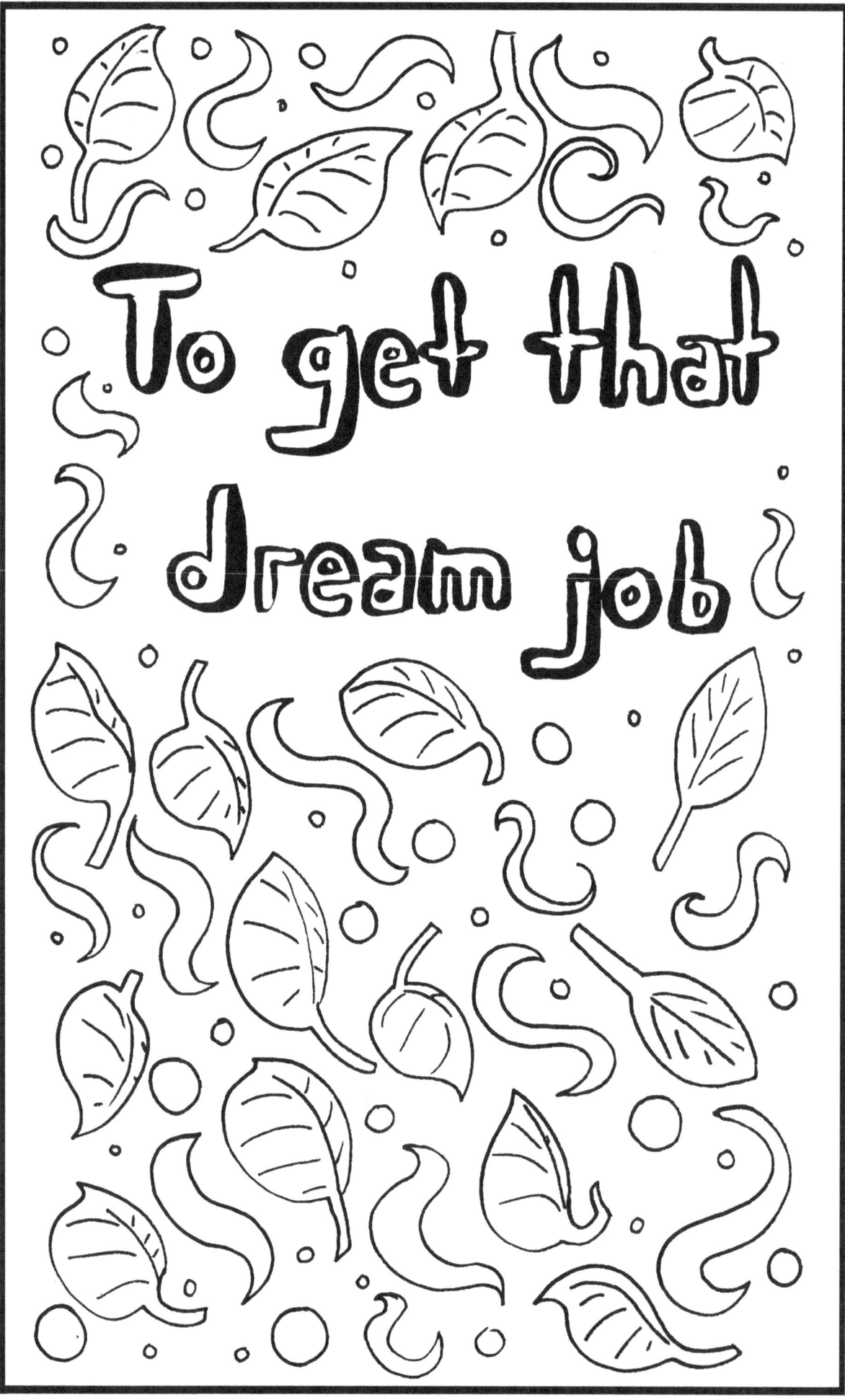

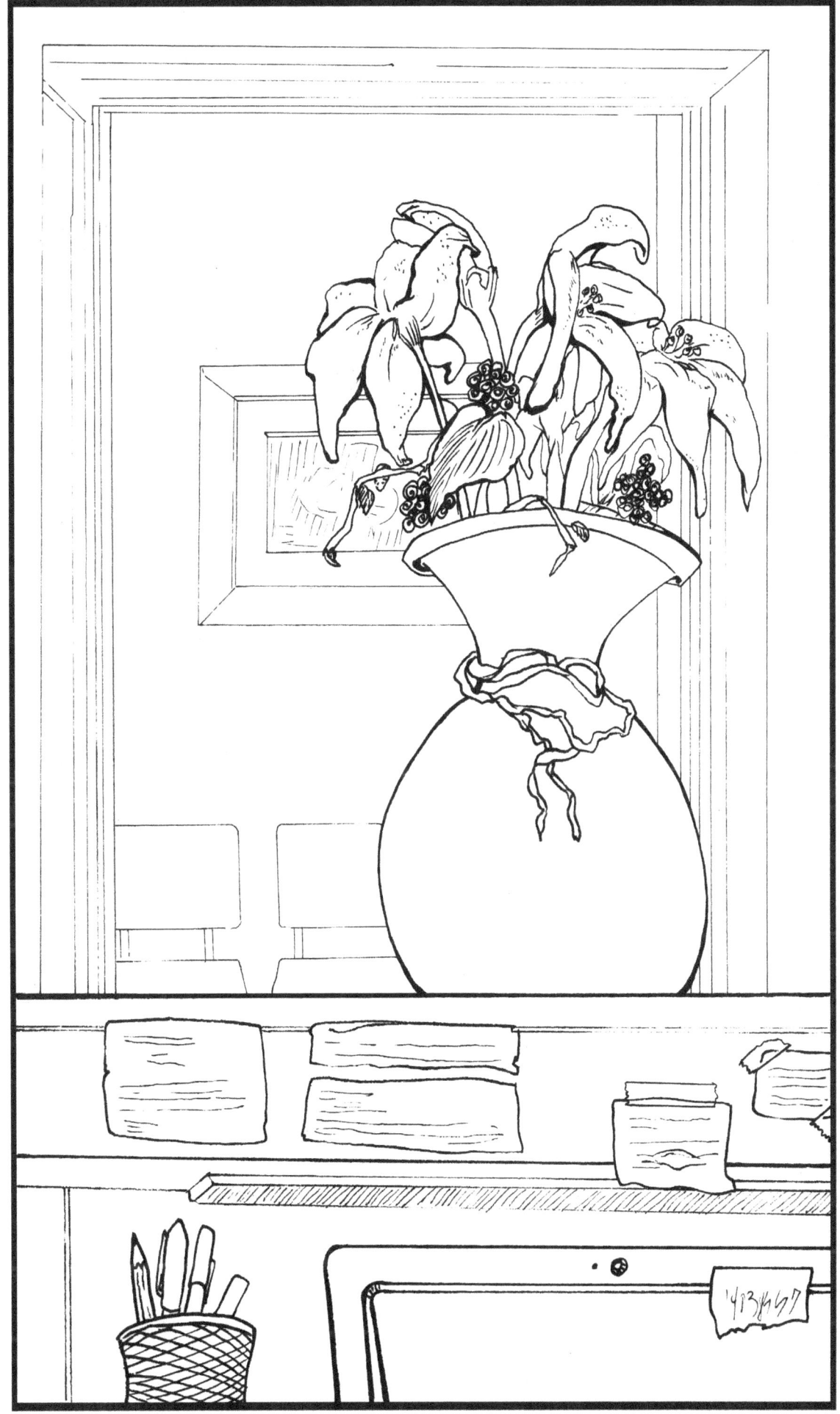

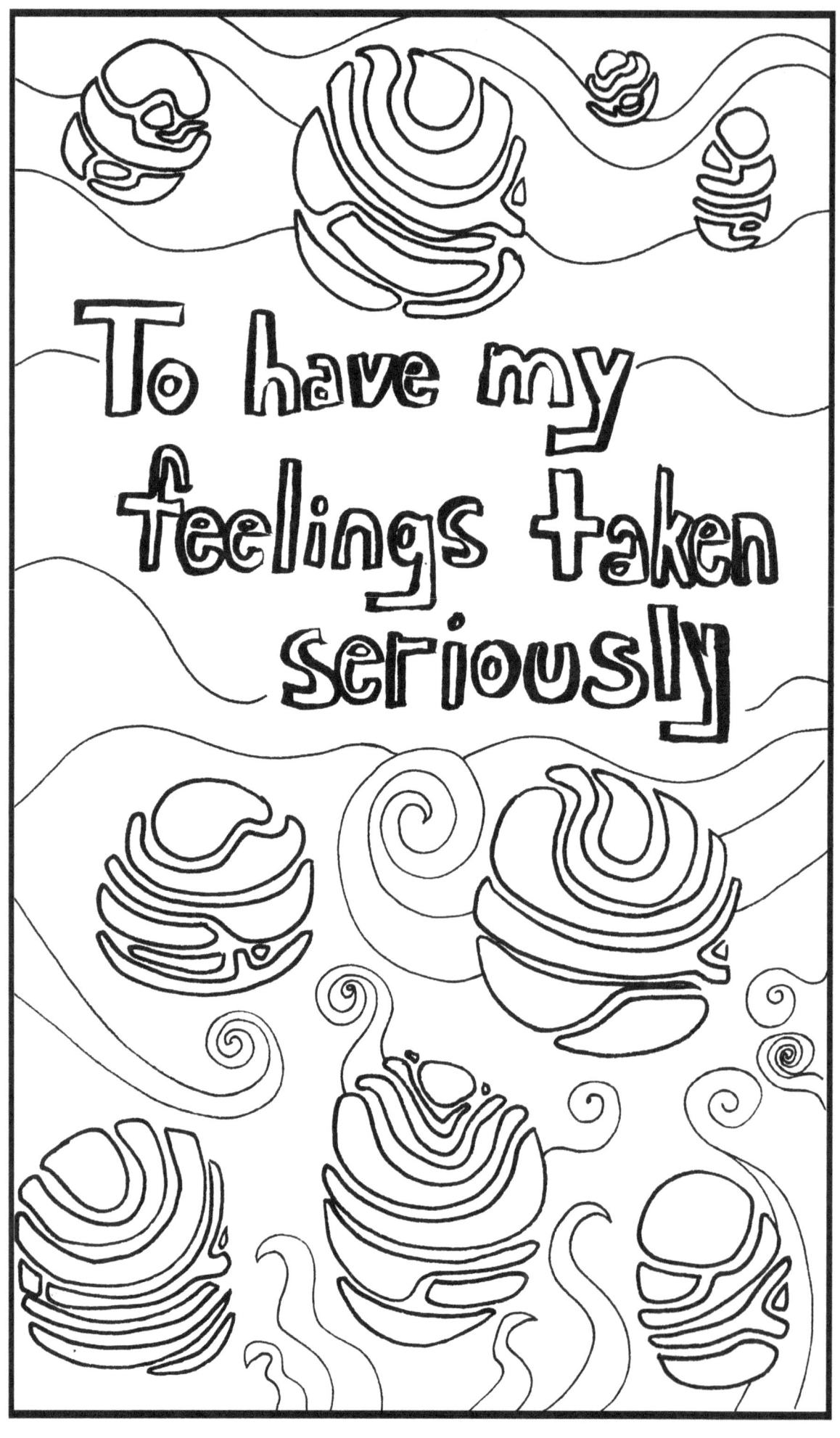

To have my
feelings taken
seriously

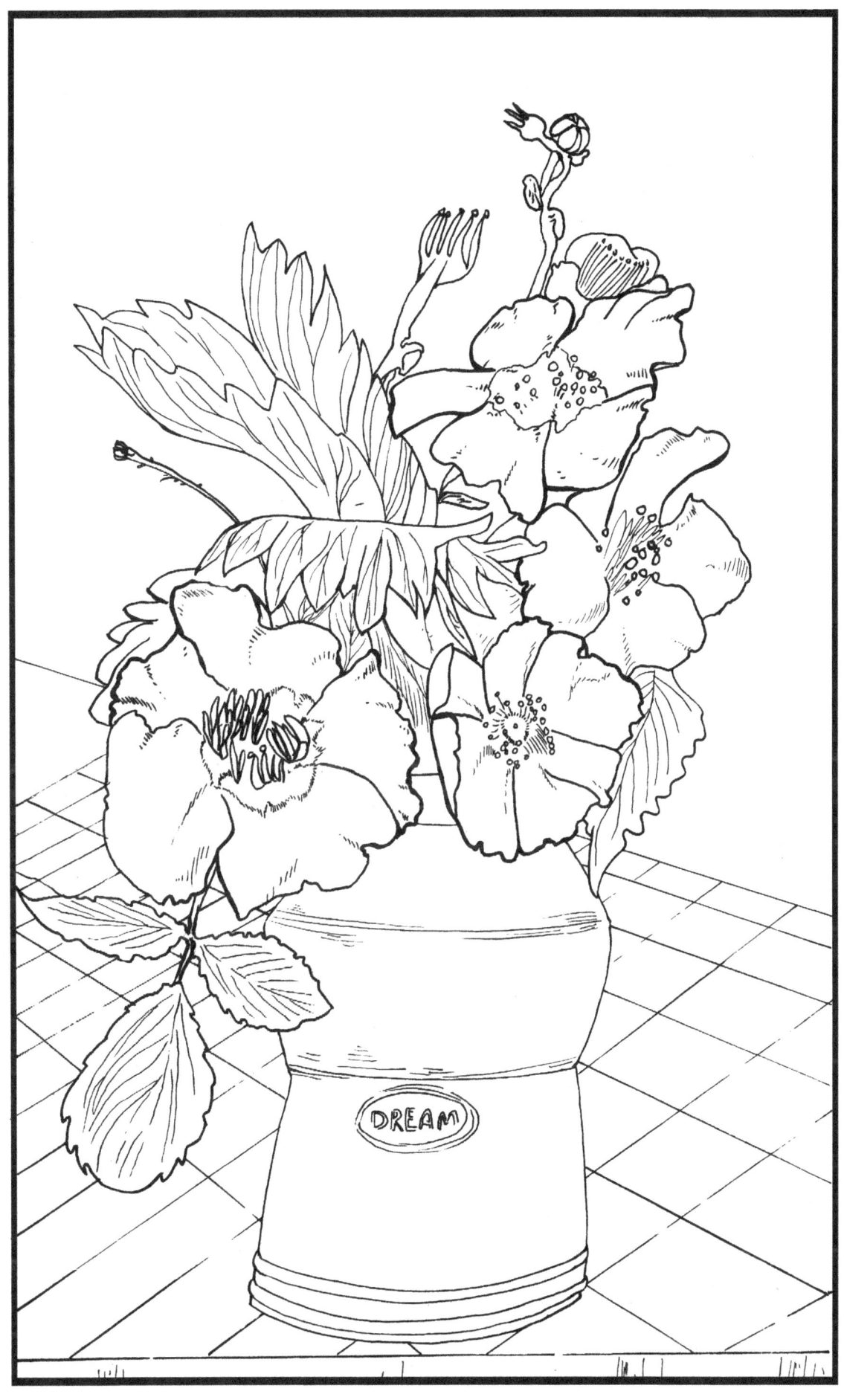

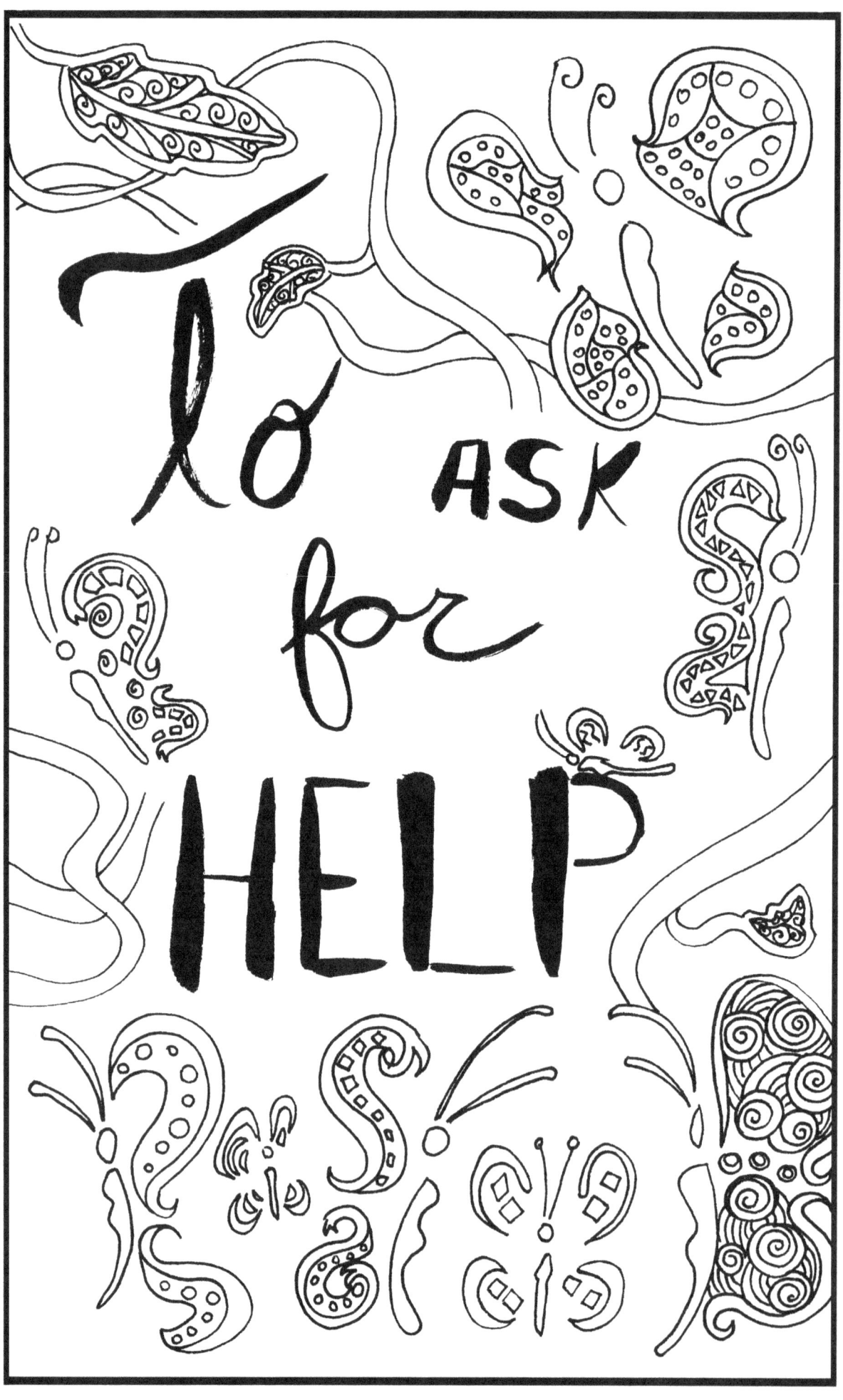

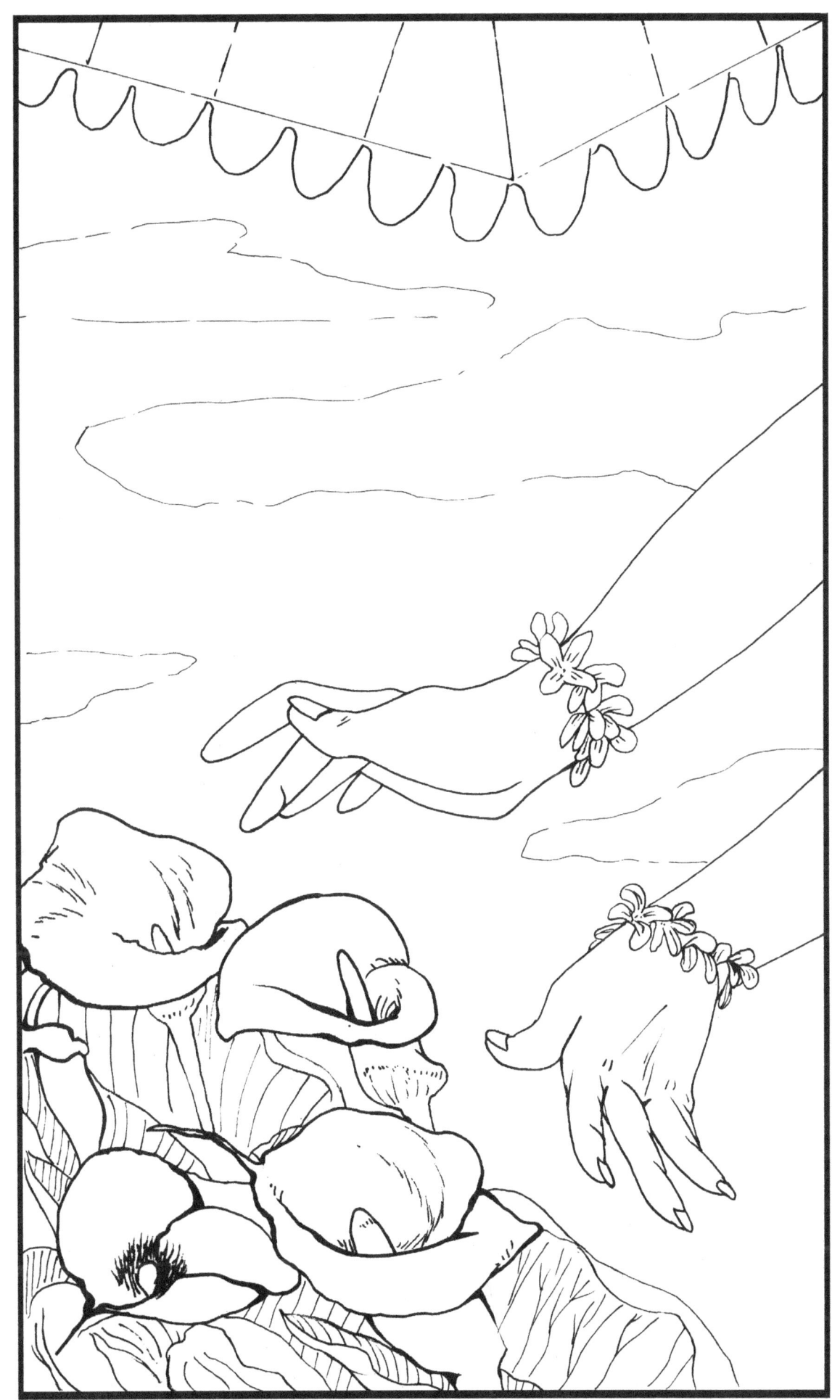

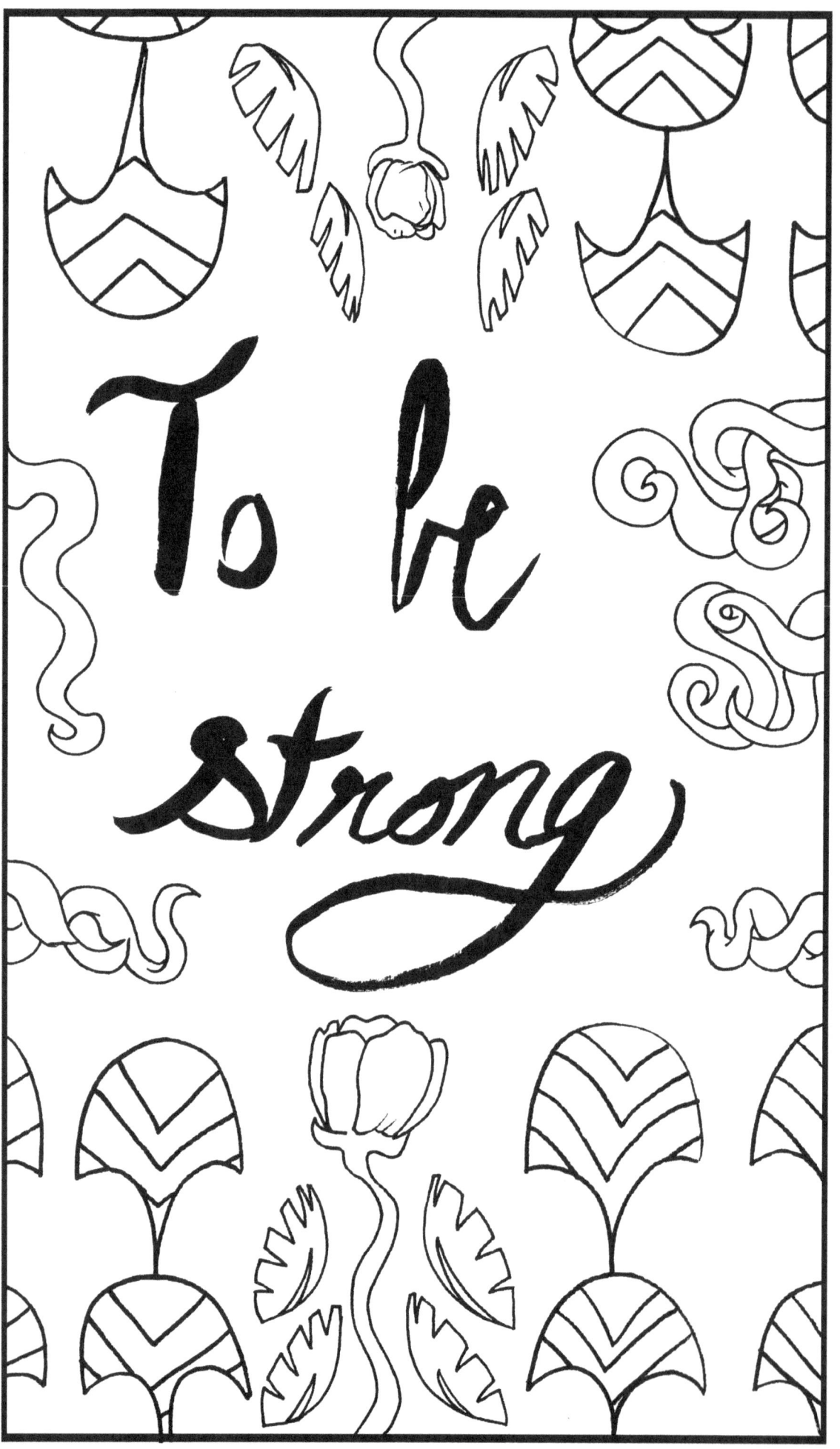

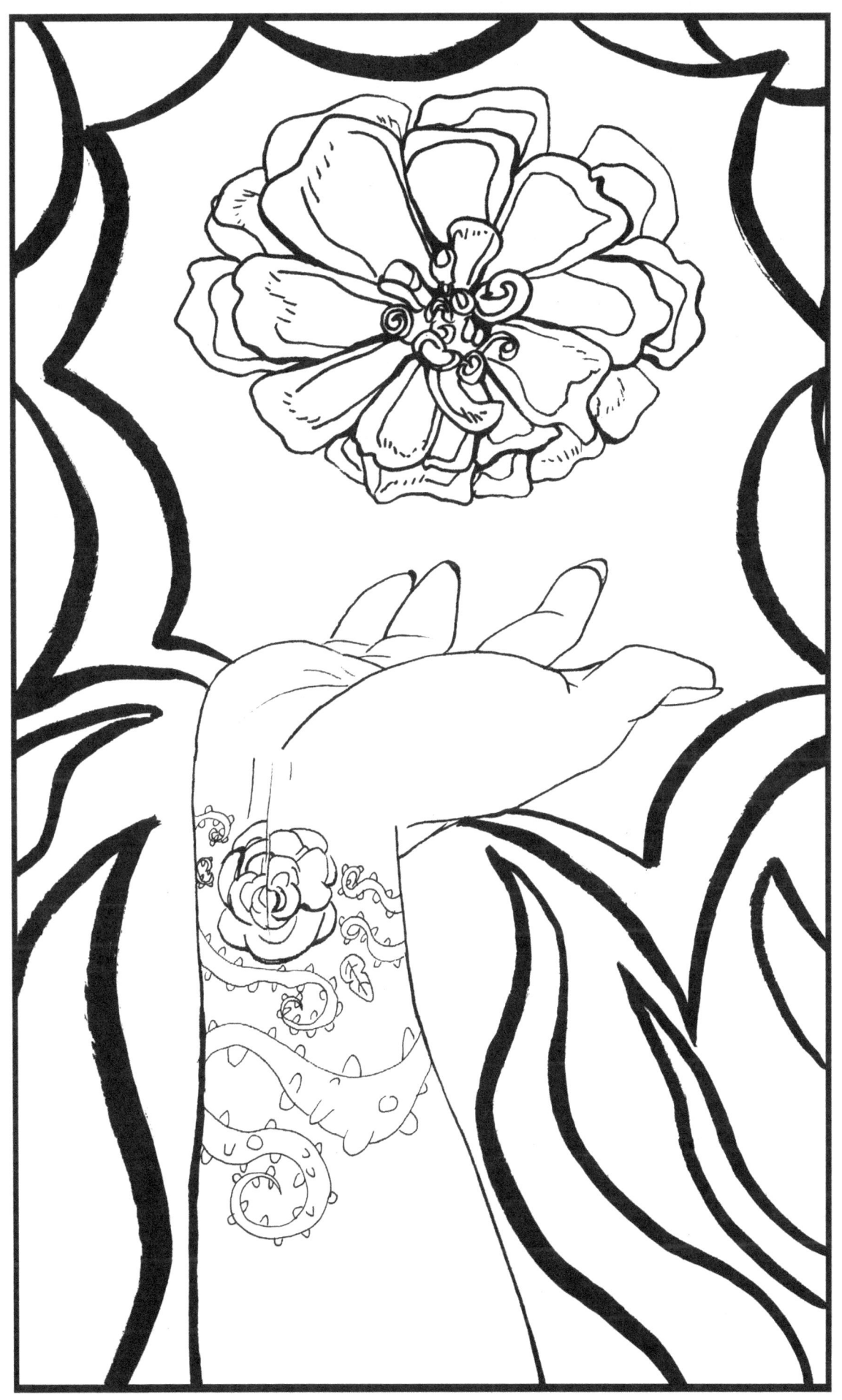

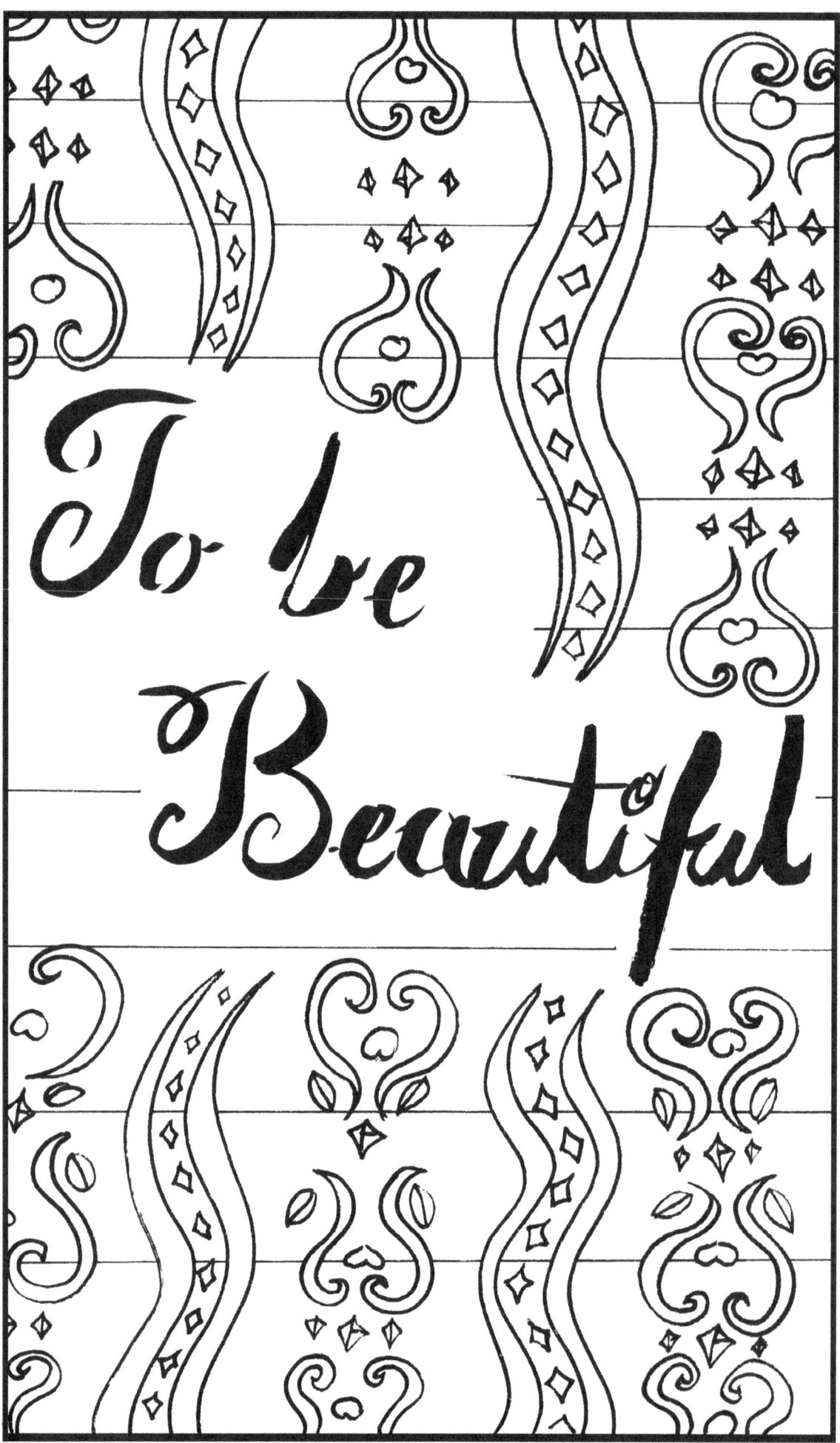

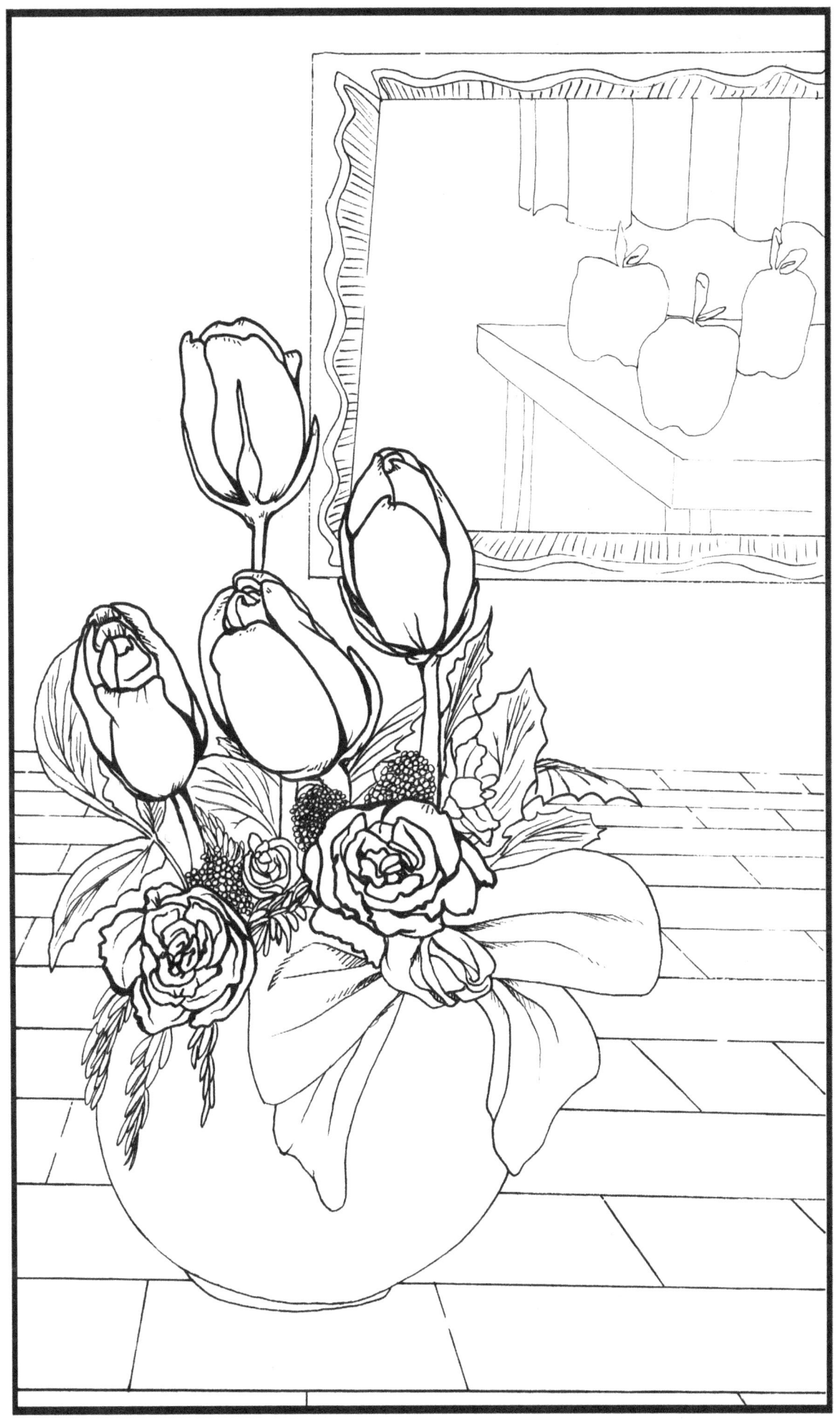

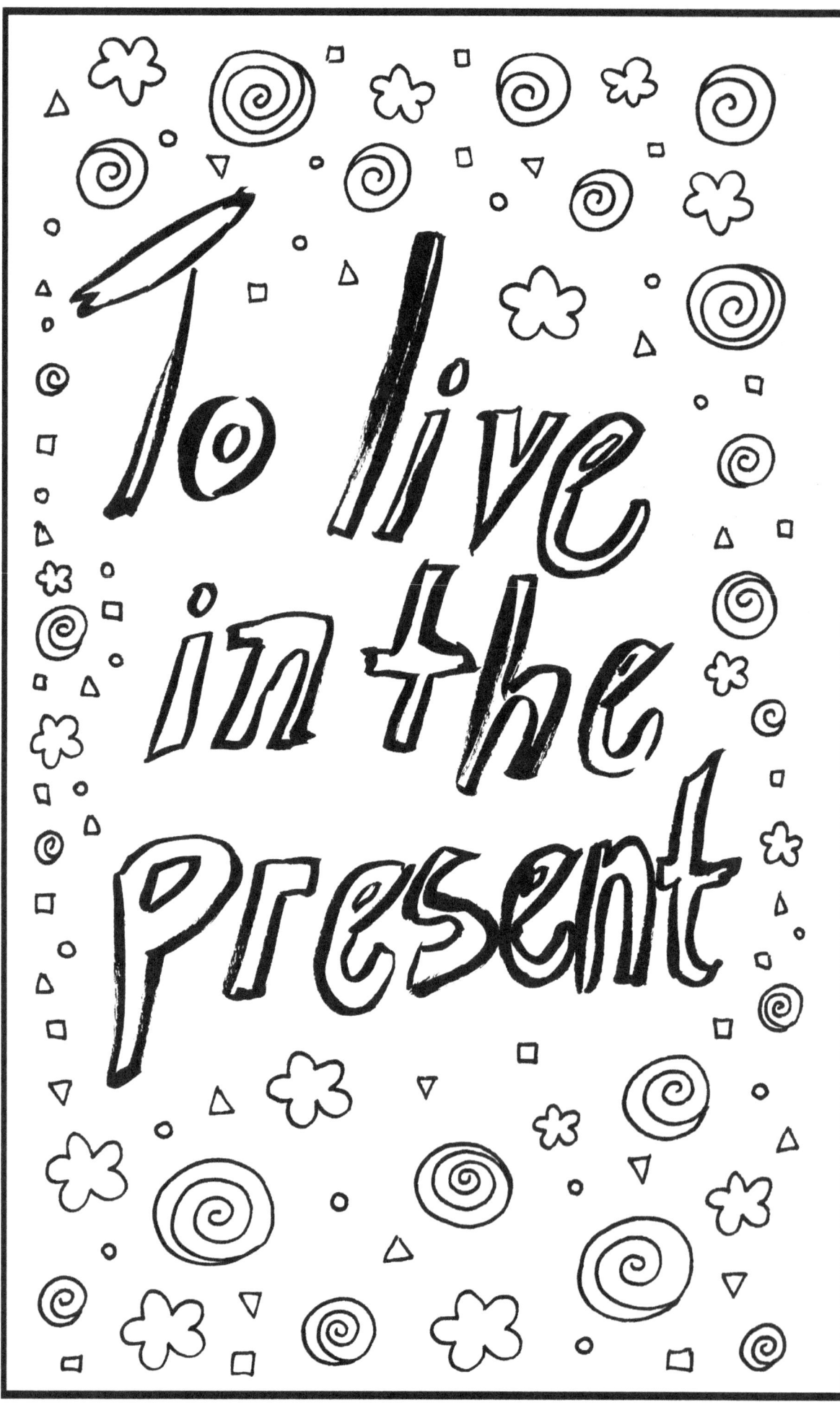

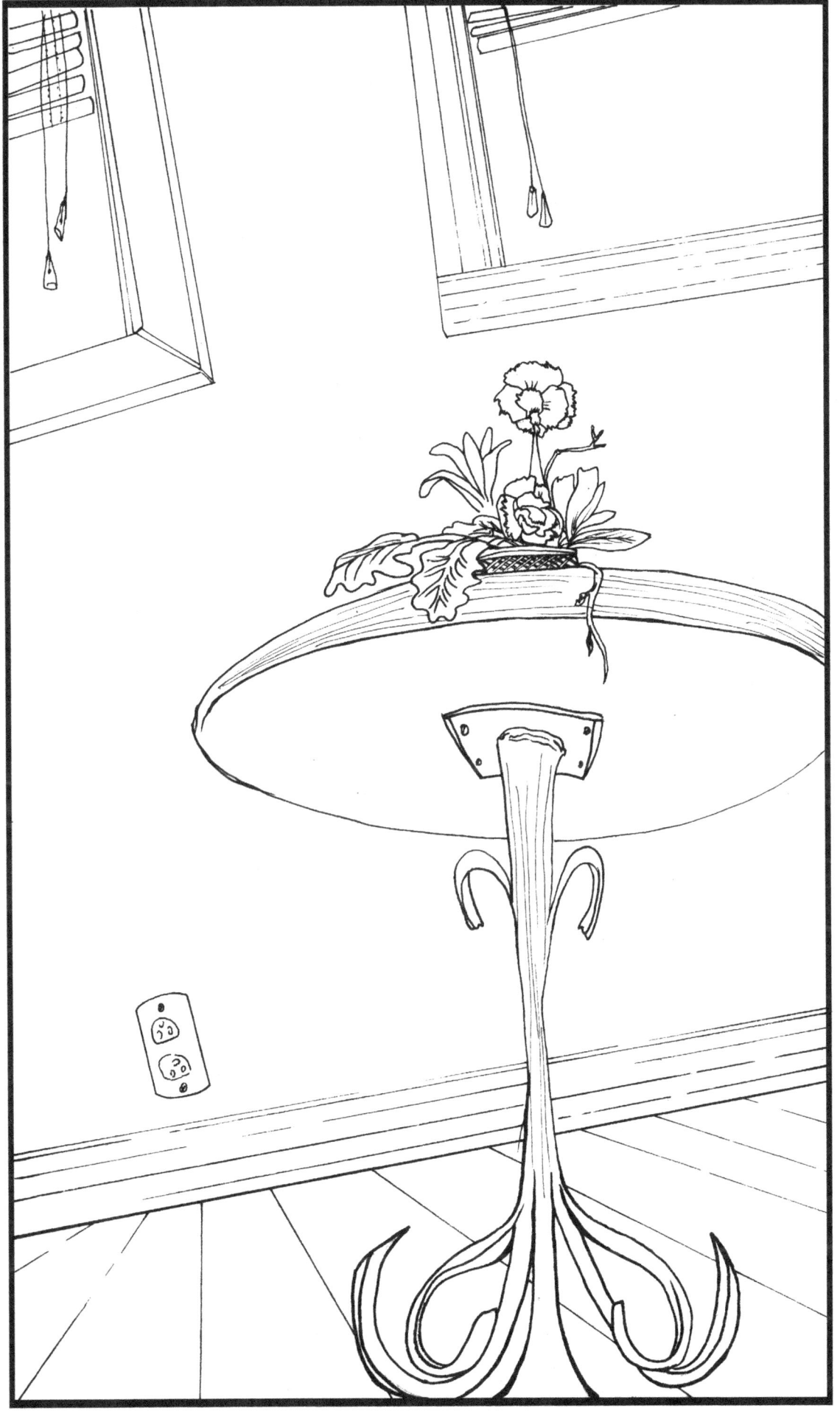

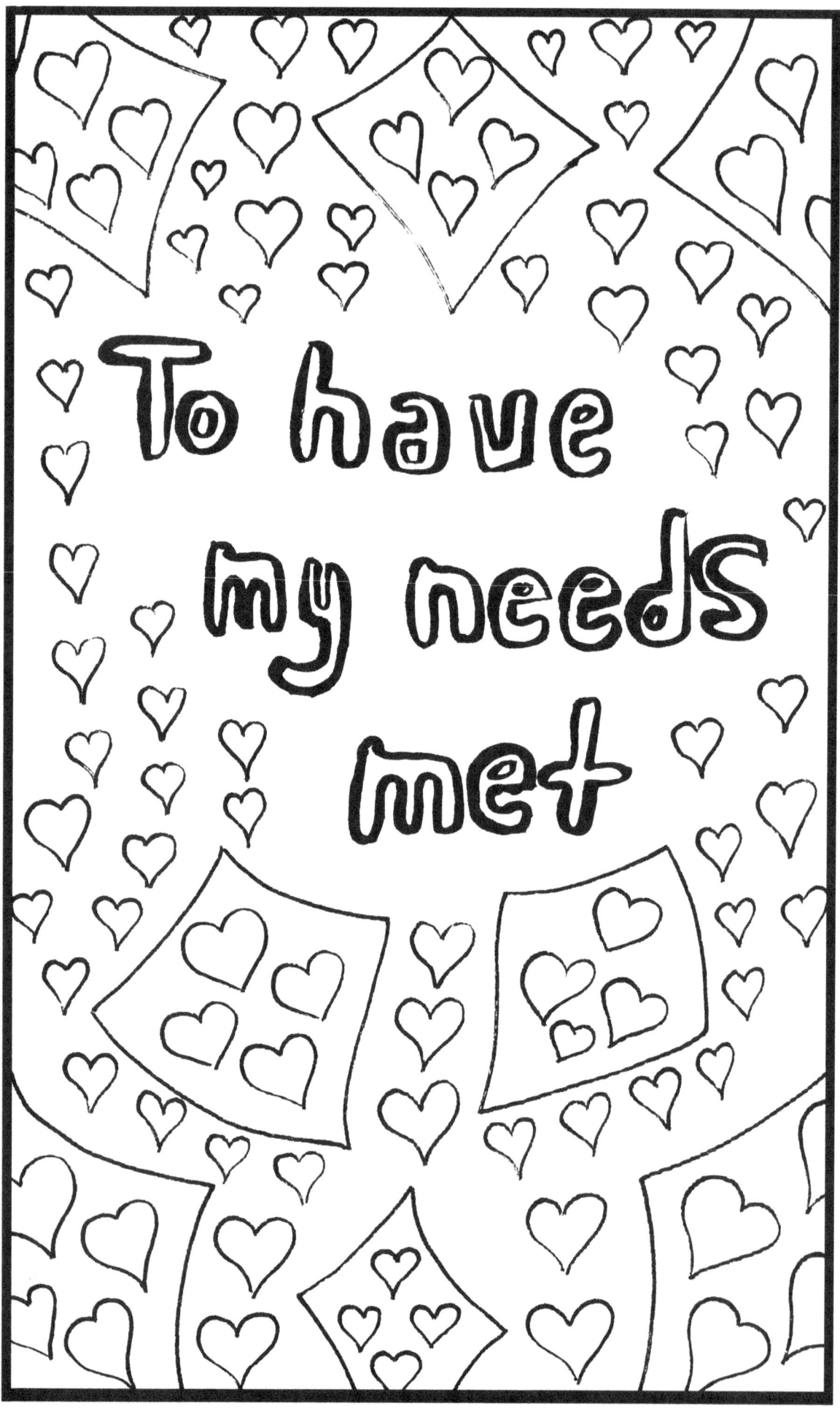

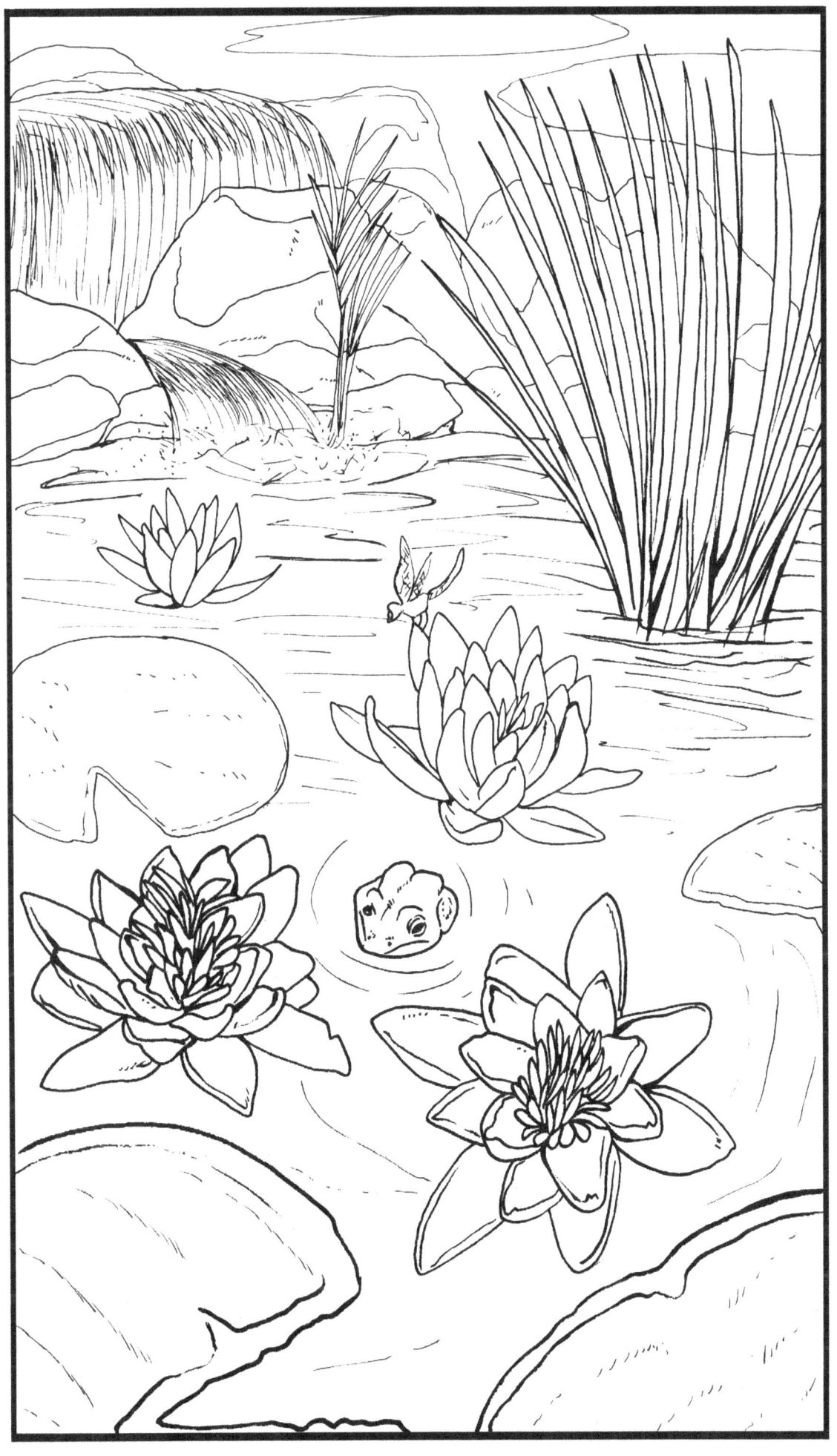

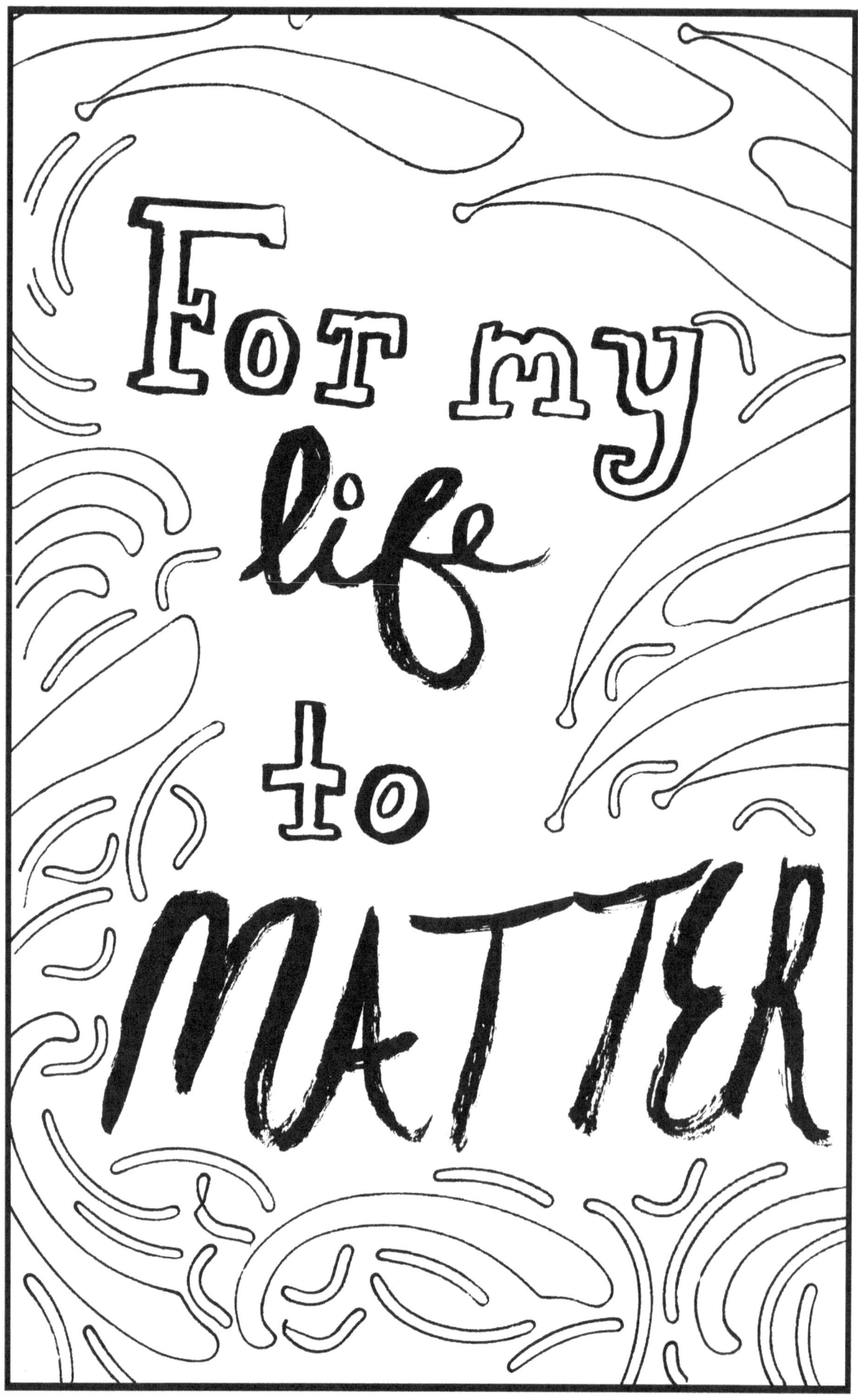

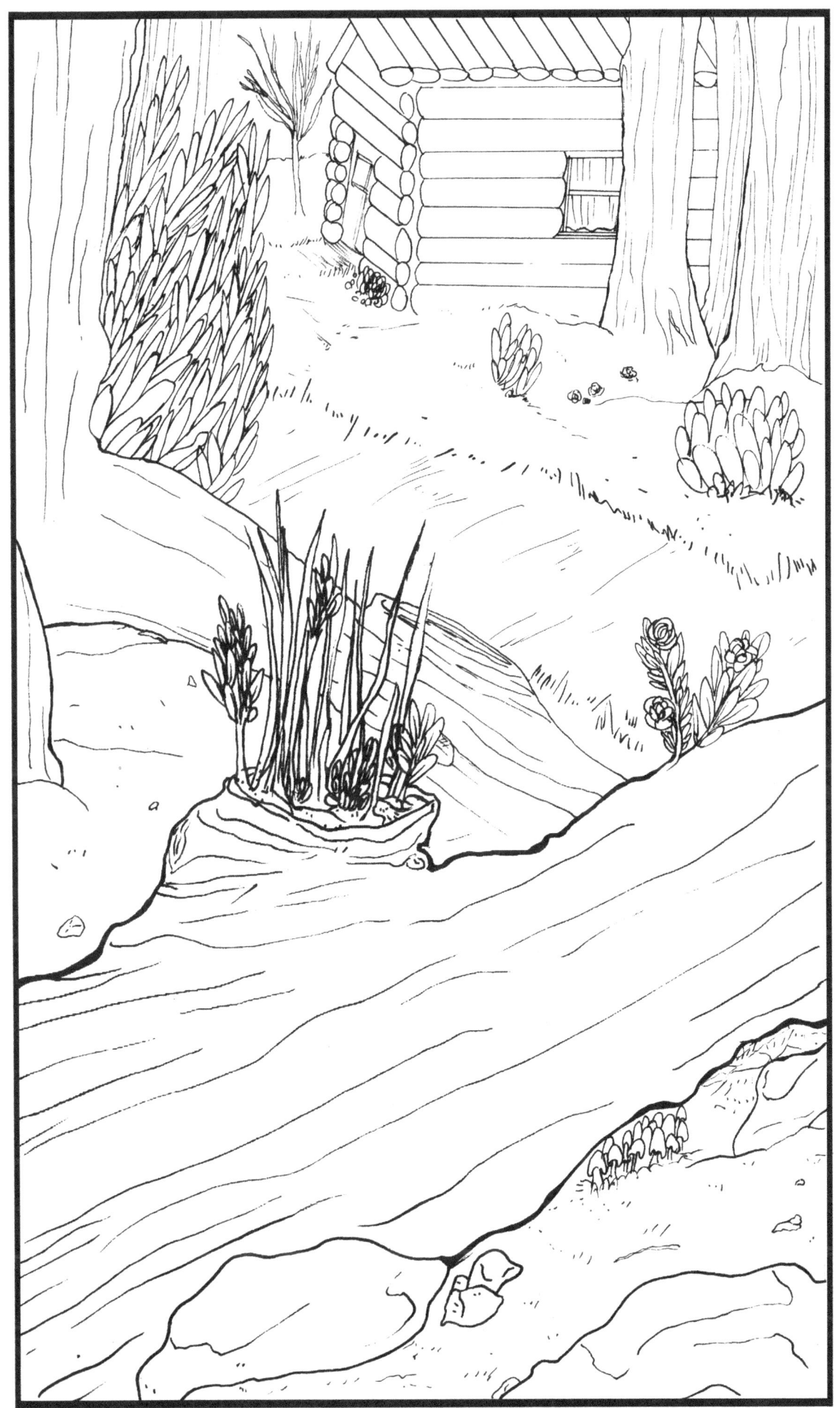

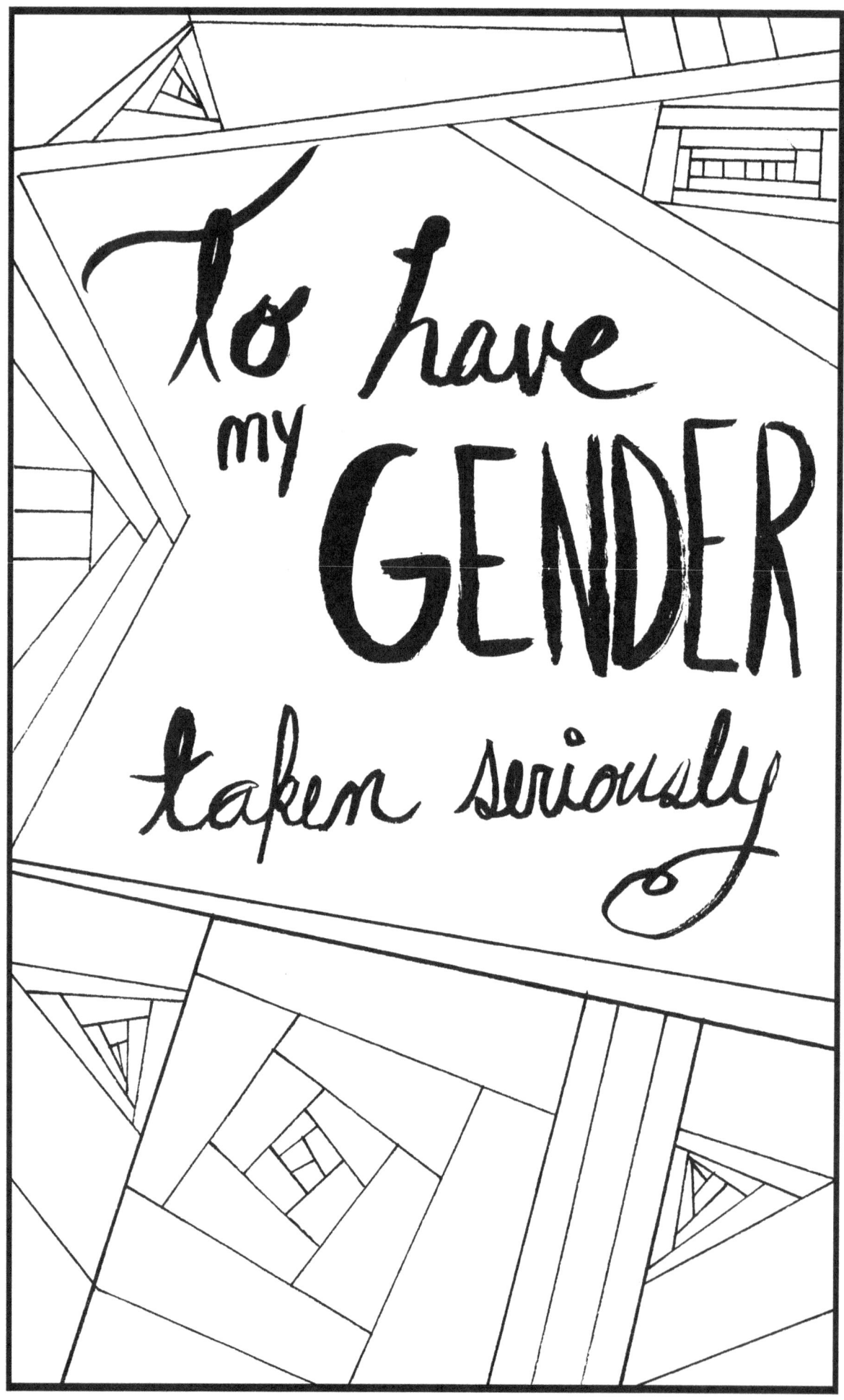

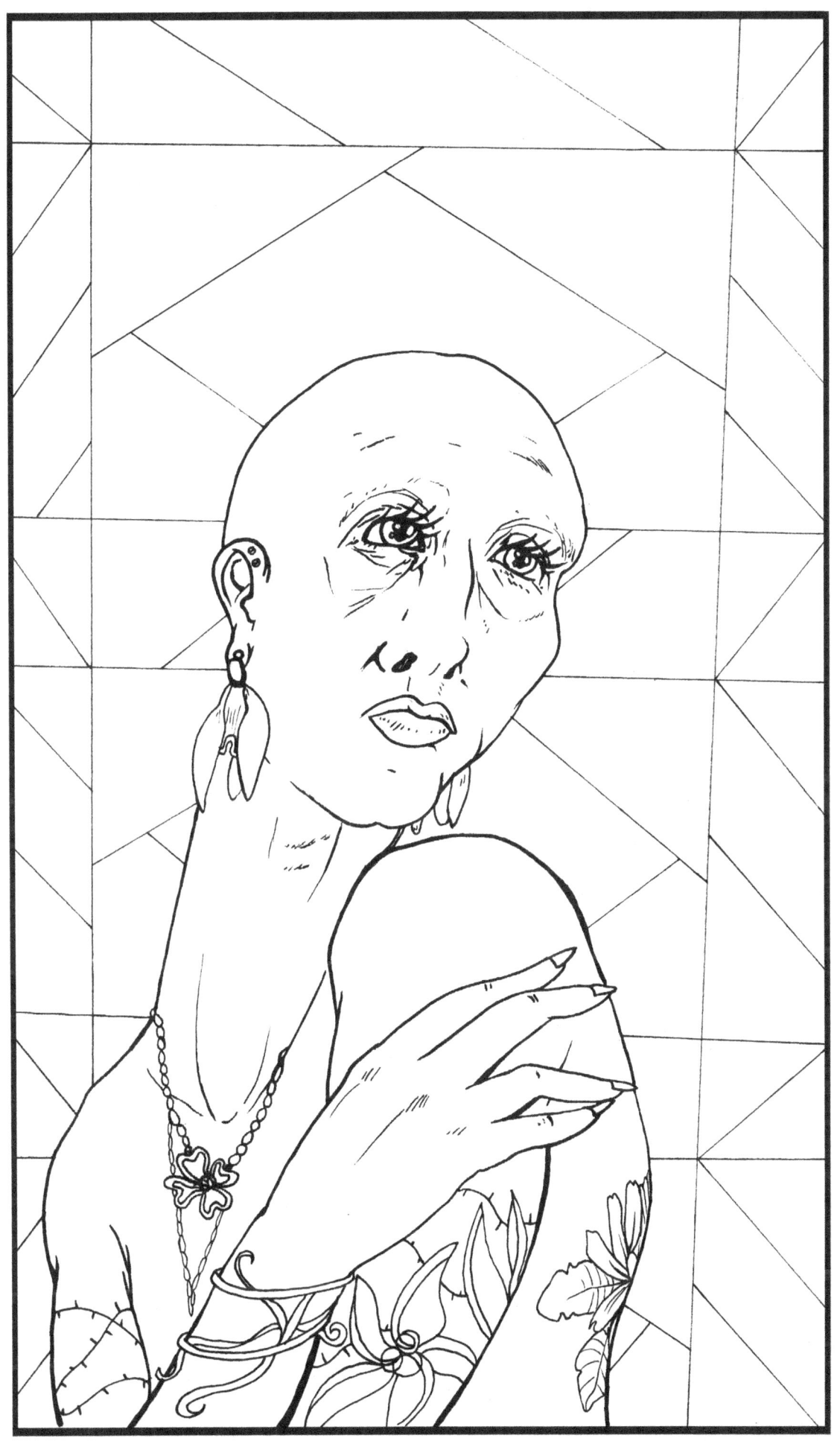

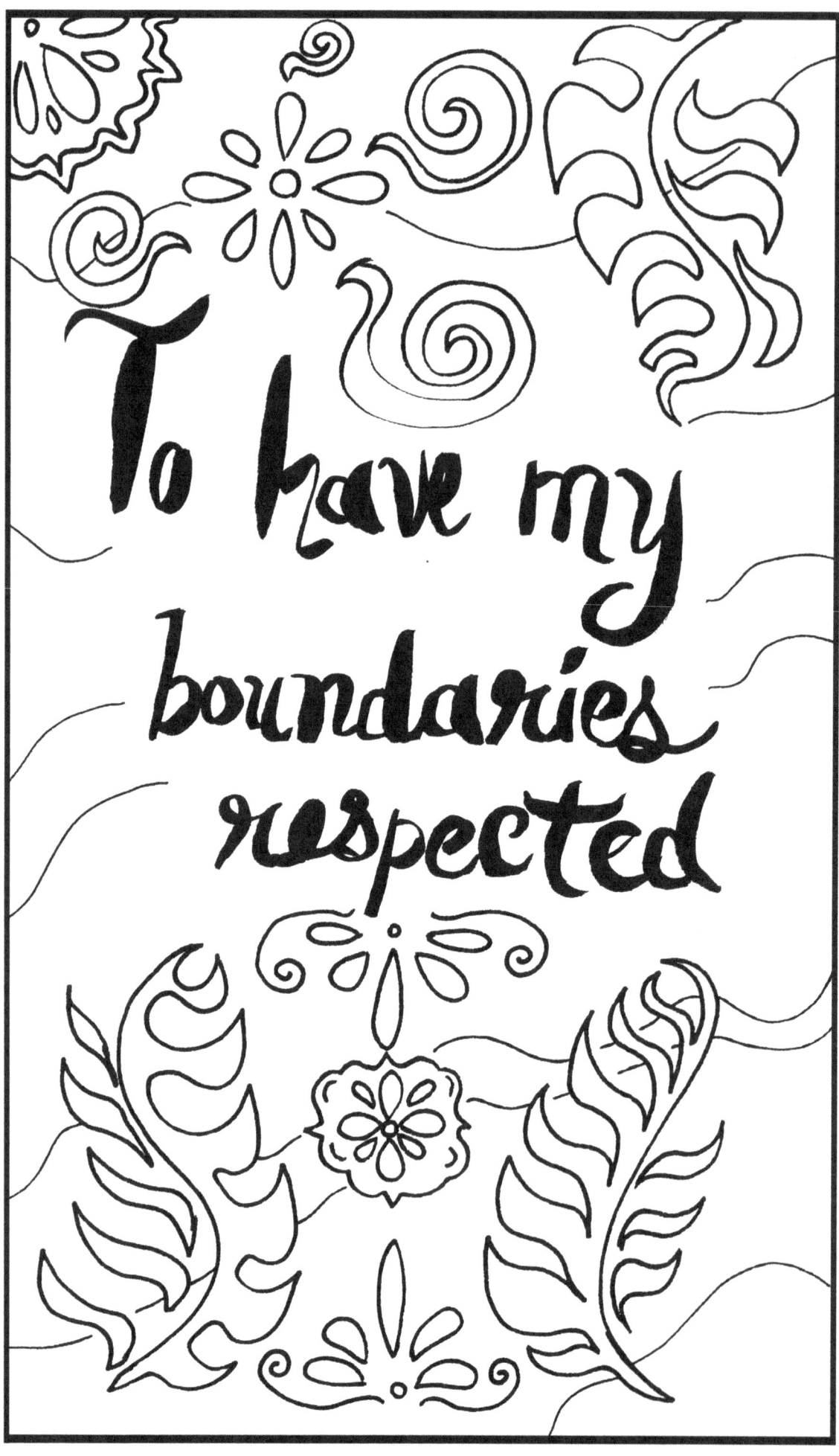

To have my boundaries respected

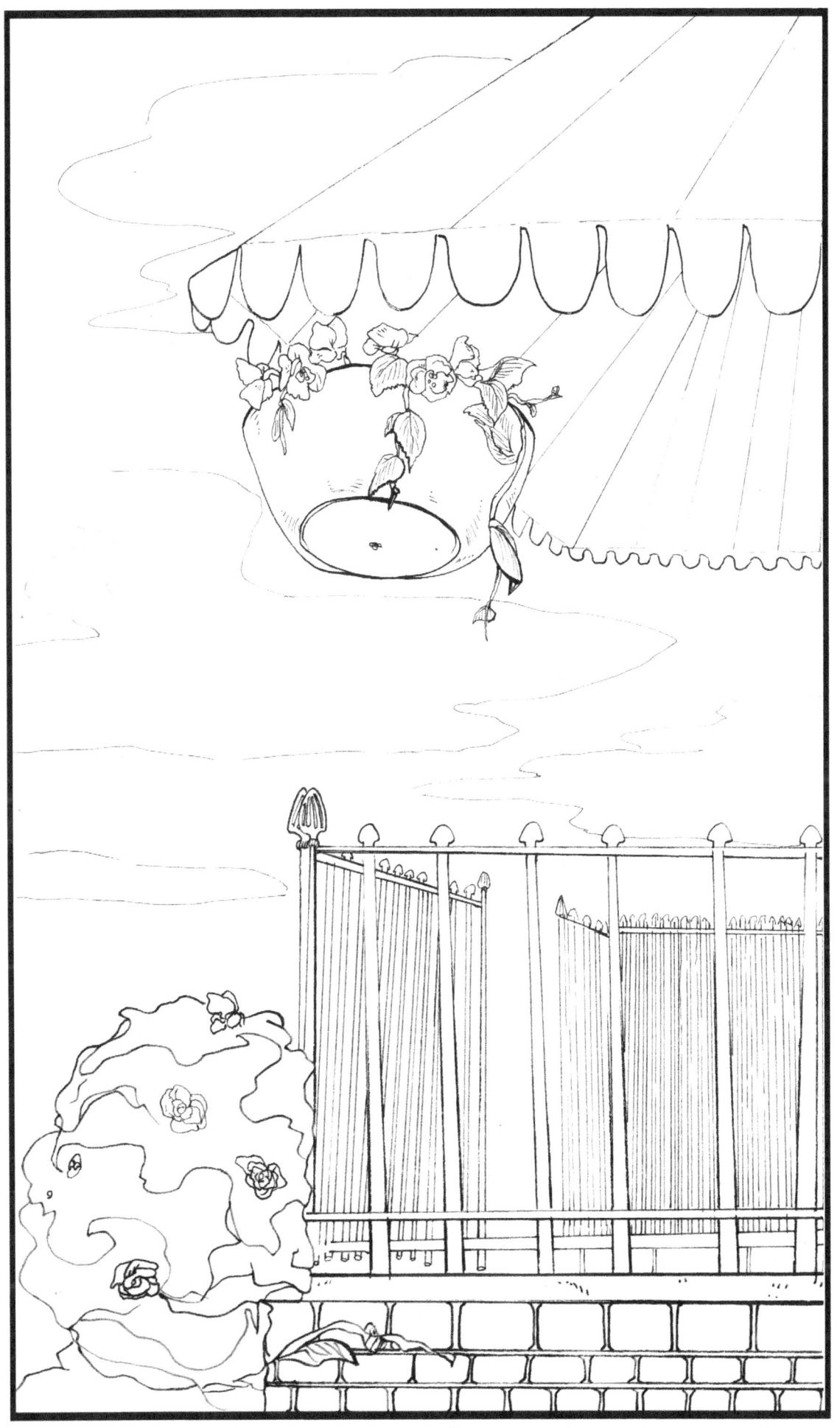

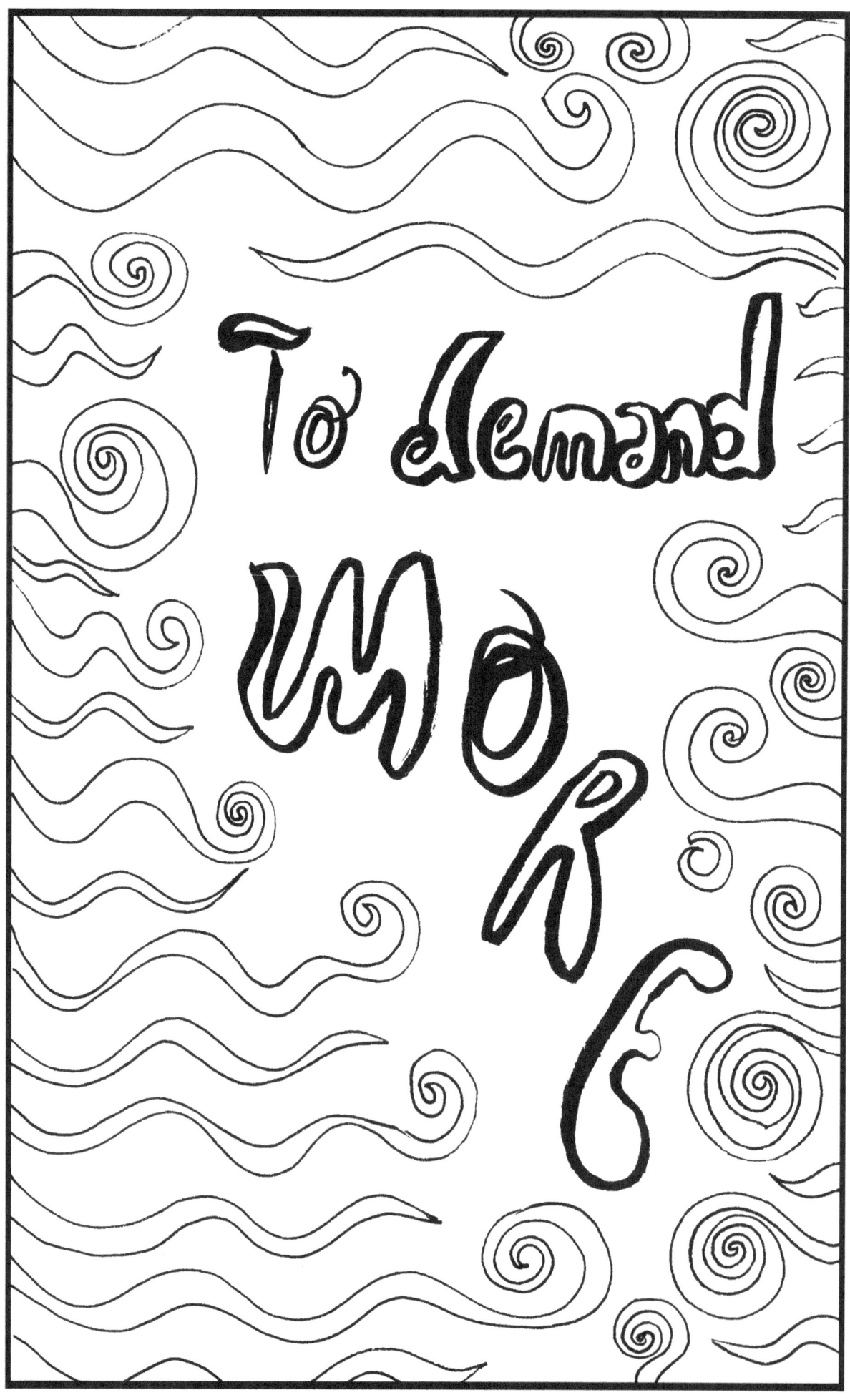

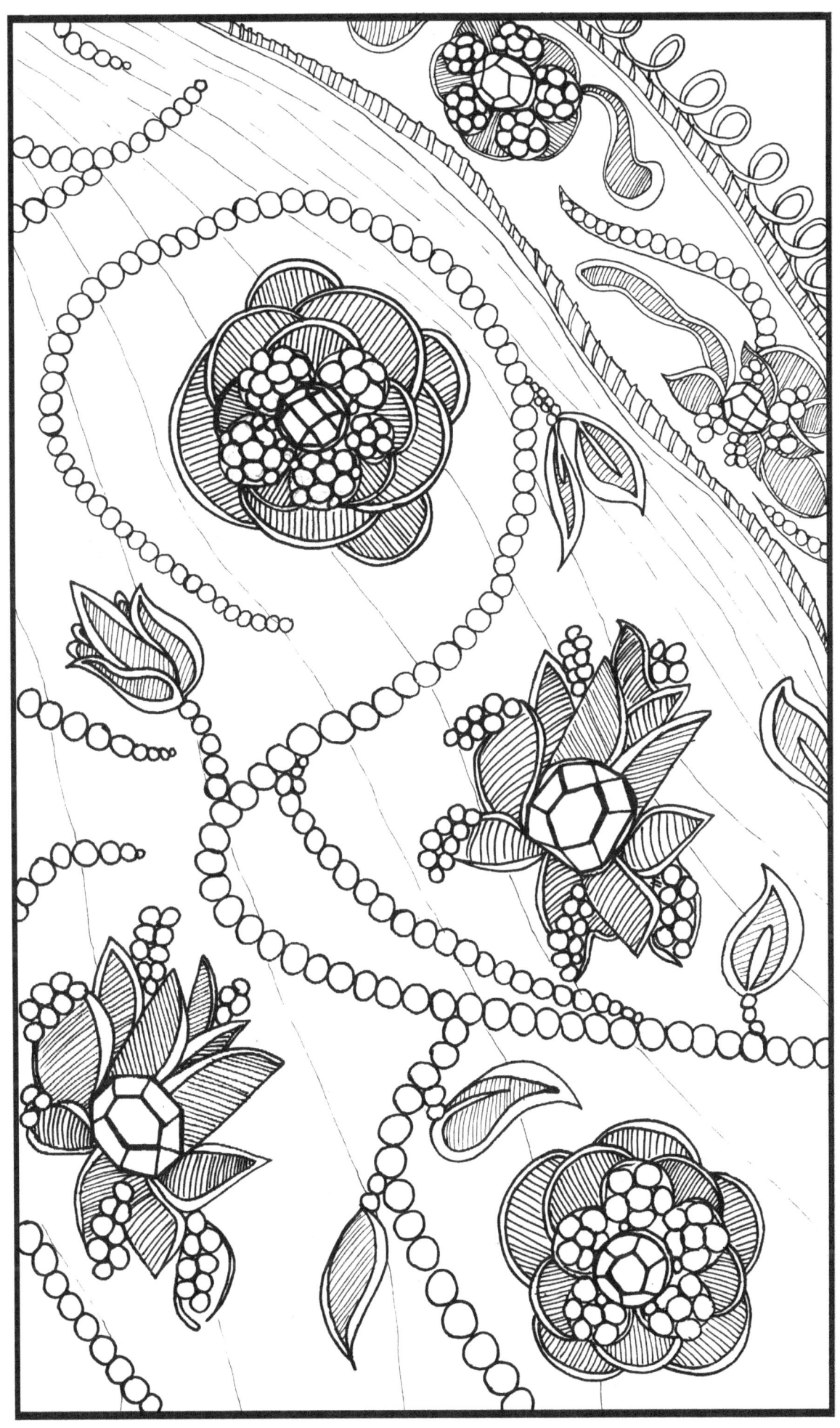

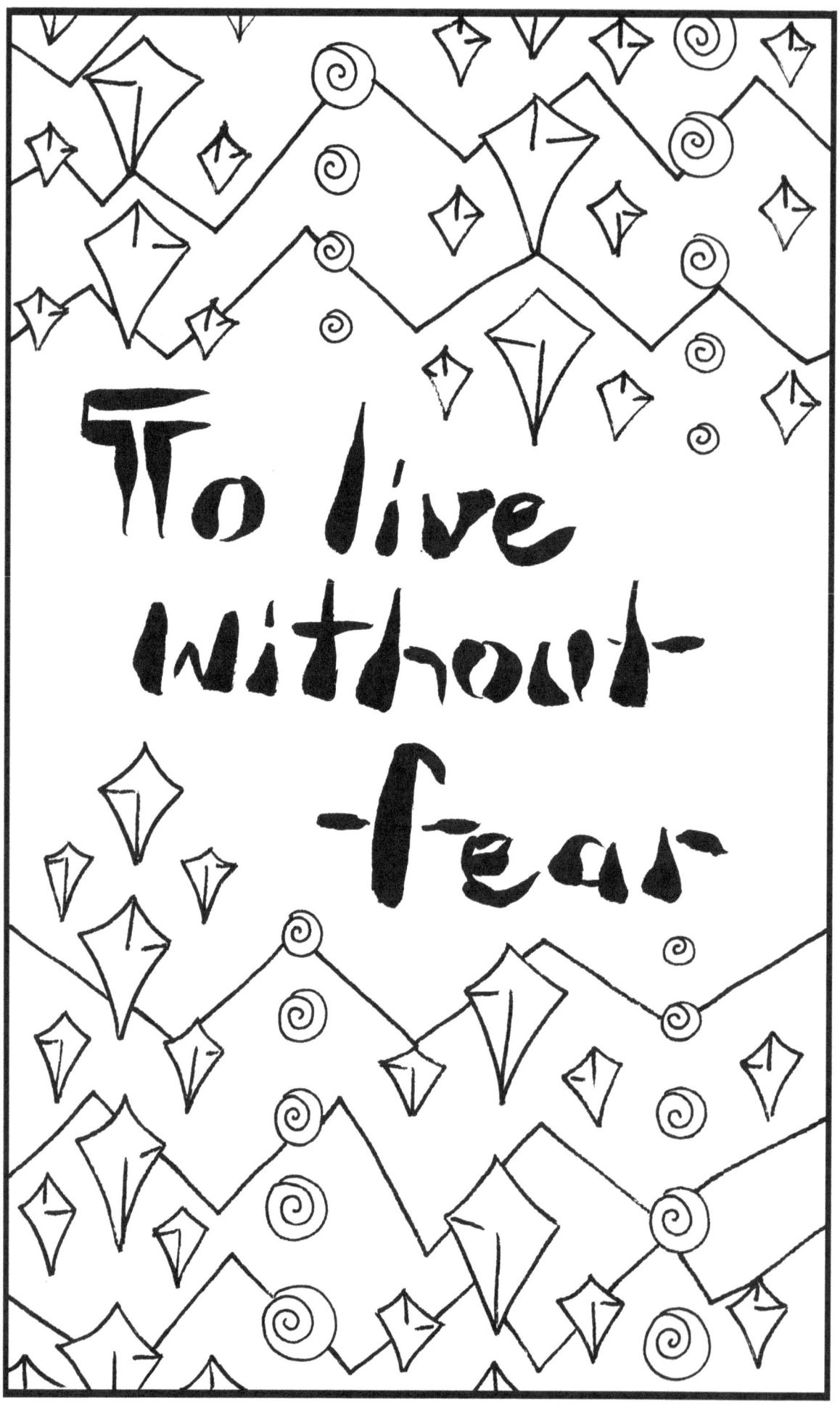

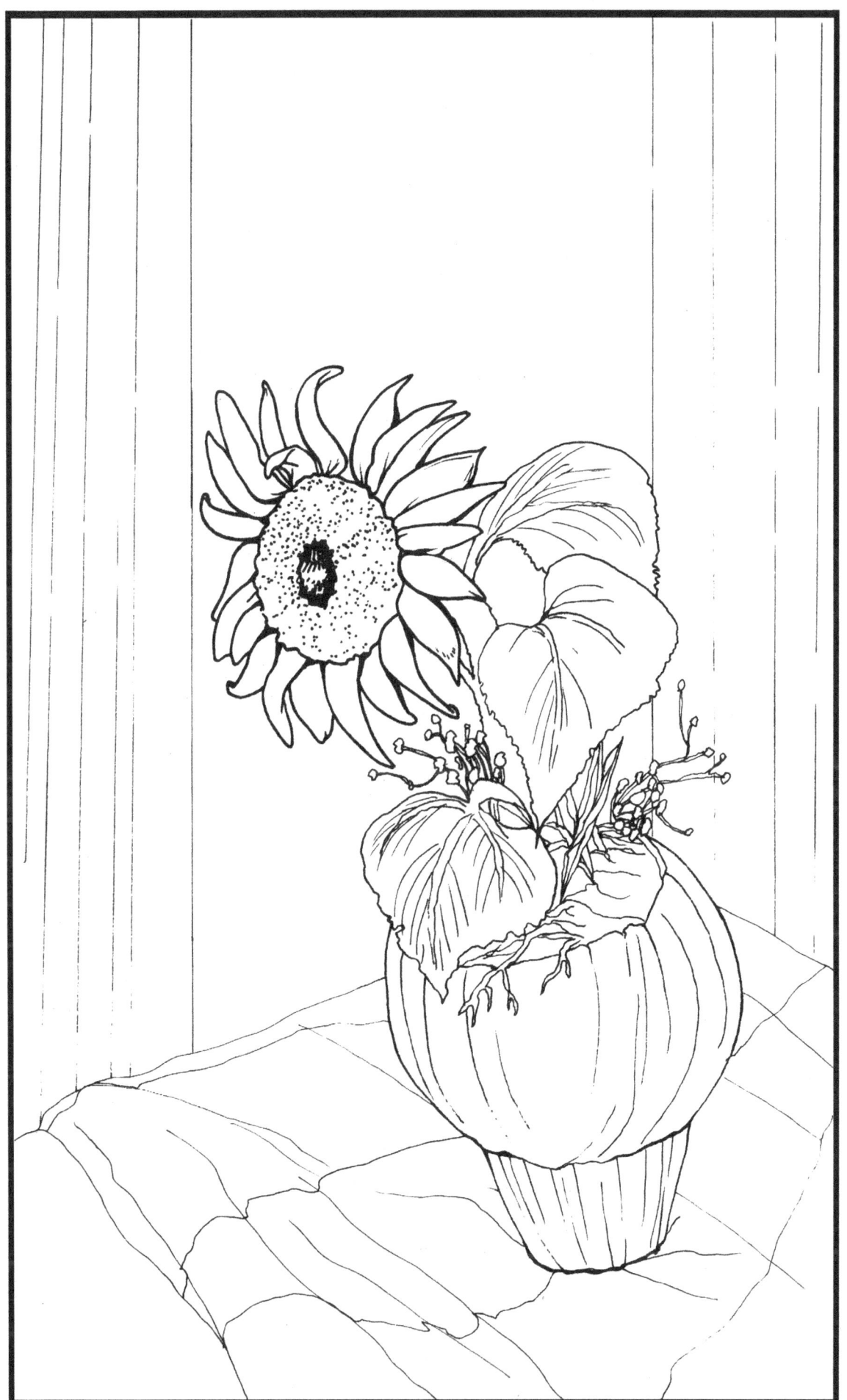

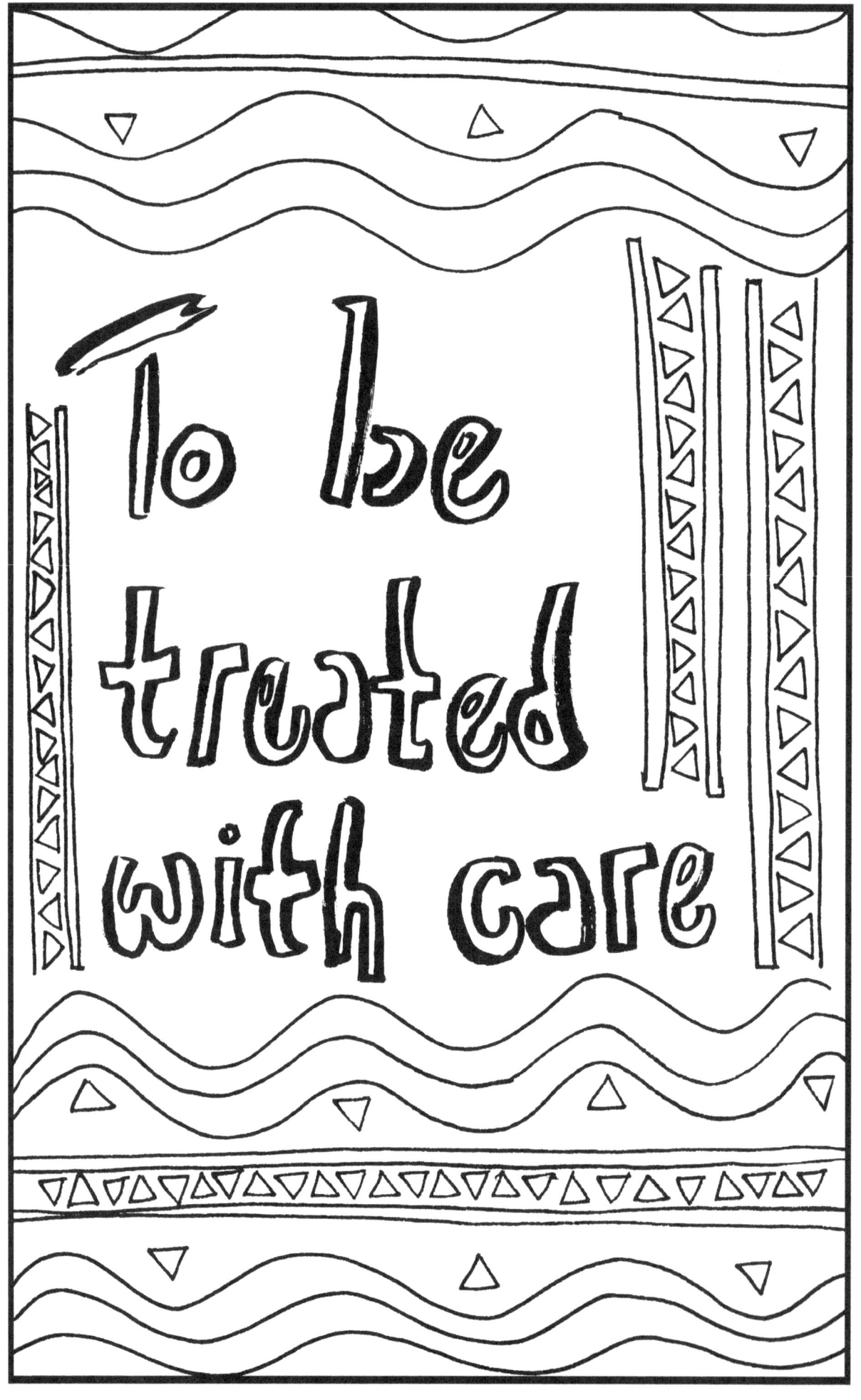

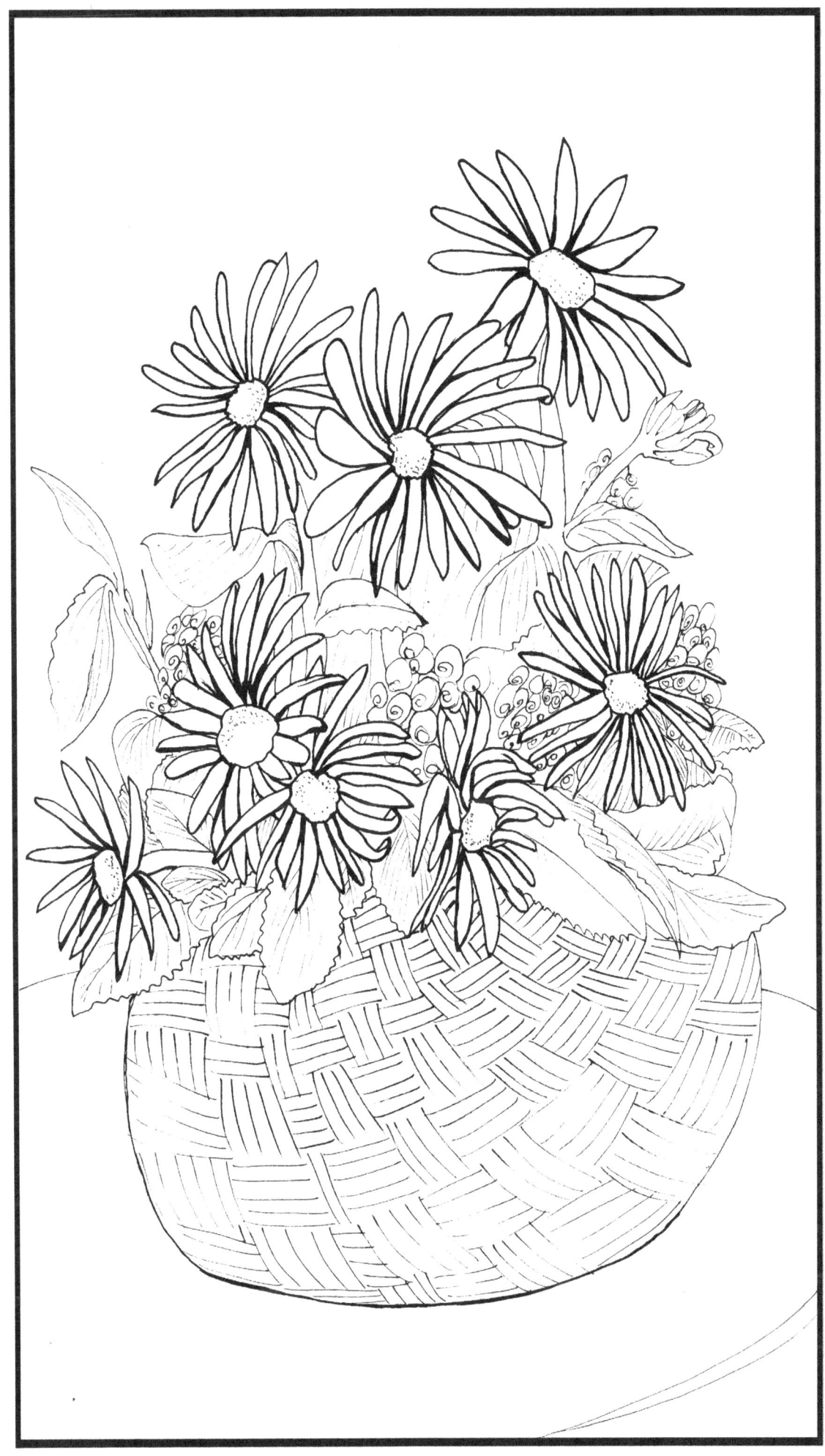

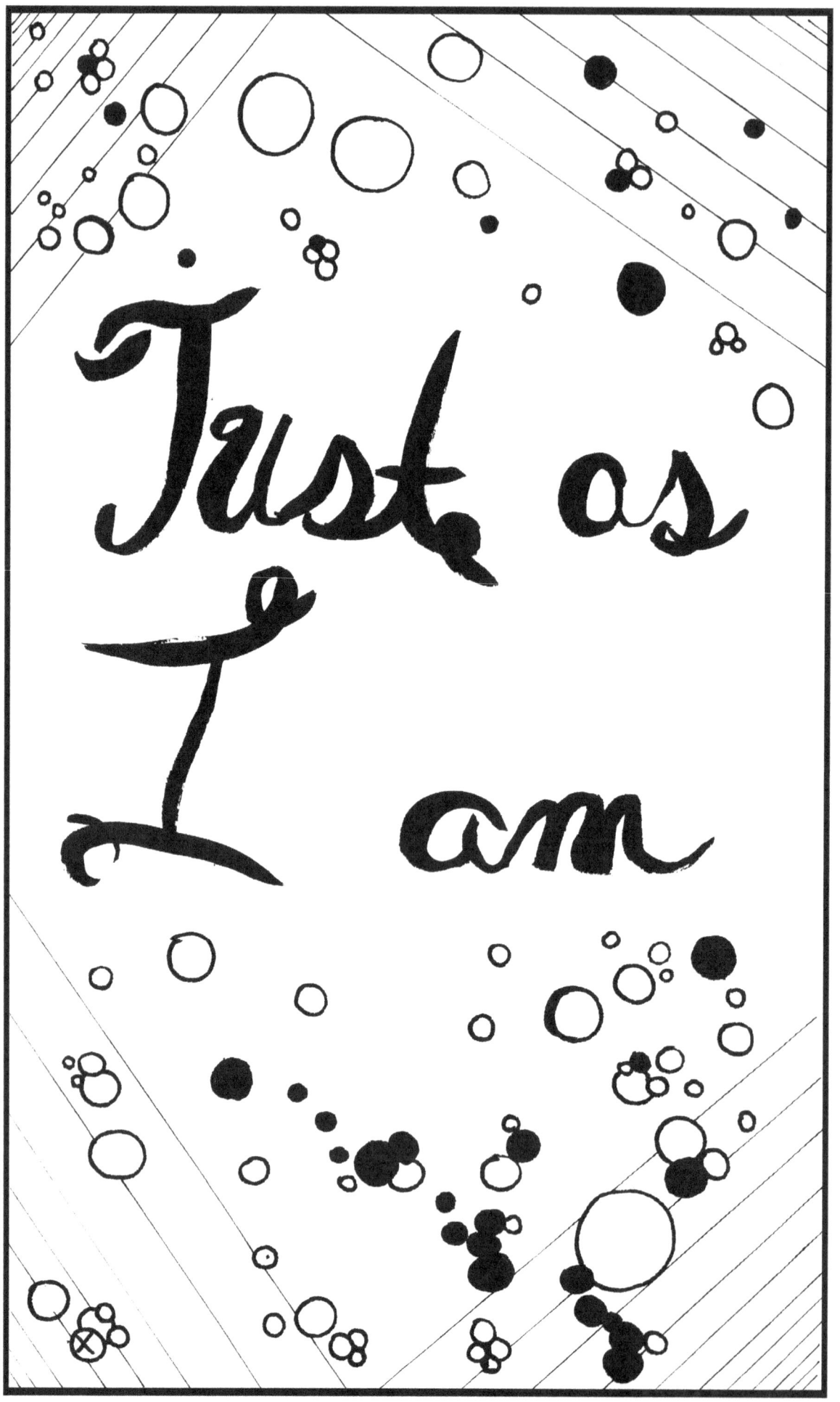

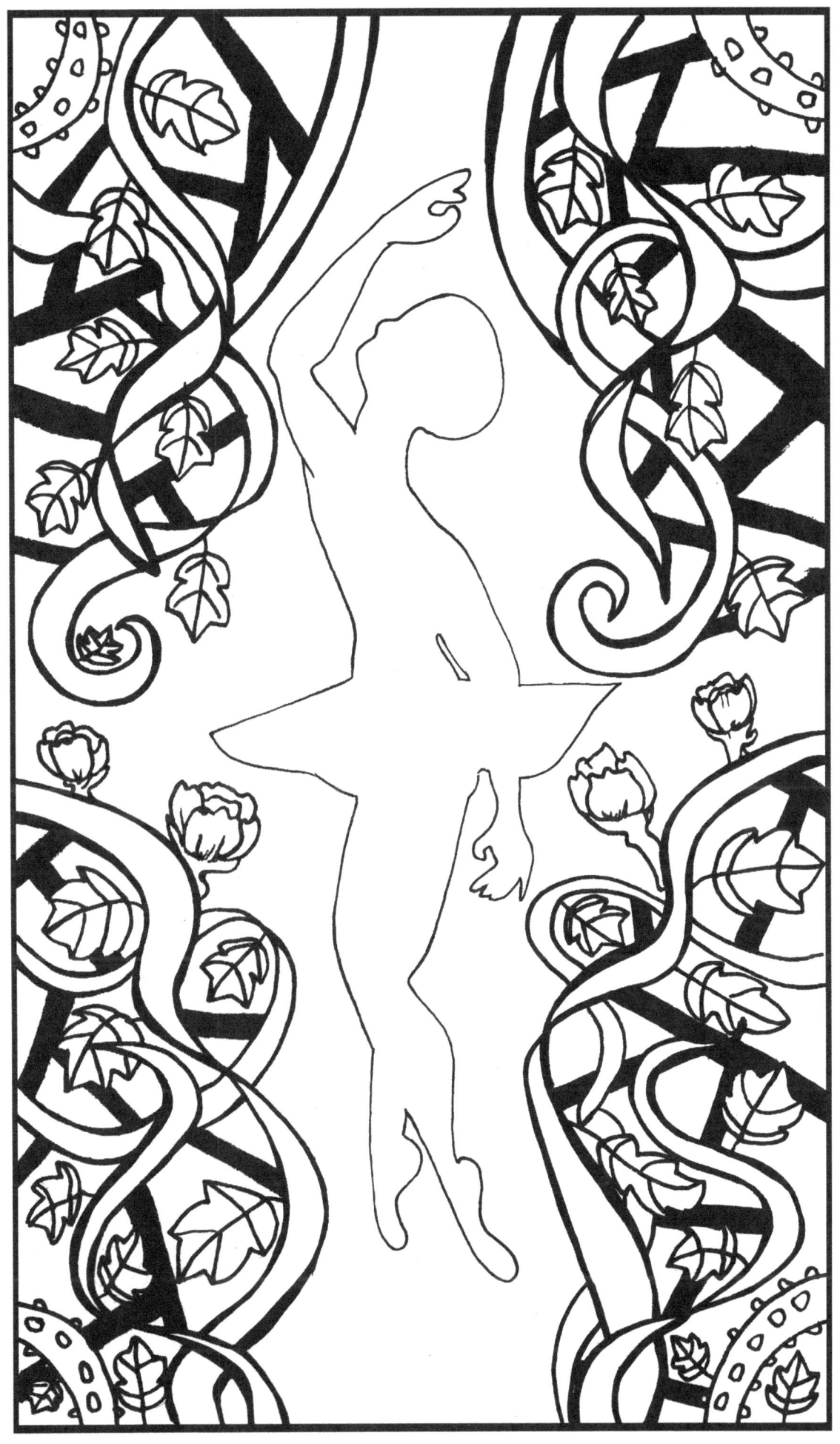

THANK YOU.